THE ABC's OF

DOLL

Collecting

THE ABC's OF DOLL Collecting

JOHN C. SCHWEITZER

Sterling Publishing Co., Inc. New York

Cover photo:

Particularly choice and beautifully
dressed French dolls. (Photograph by
Matt Christ. Courtesy of Auctions By
Theriault. Annapolis, Md.)

Library of Congress Cataloging in Publication Data

Schweitzer, John C.
   The ABC's of doll collecting.
   Bibliography: p.
   Includes index.
   1. Dolls—Collectors and collecting.   I. Title.
NK4893.S36   688.7'221'075   81-8764
ISBN 0-8069-5428-0   AACR2
ISBN 0-8069-5429-9 (lib. bdg.)

Second Printing, 1982

Copyright © 1981 by Sterling Publishing Co., Inc.
Two Park Avenue, New York, N.Y. 10016
Distributed in Australia by Oak Tree Press Co., Ltd.
P.O. Box K514 Haymarket, Sydney 2000, N.S.W.
Distributed in the United Kingdom by Blandford Press
Link House, West Street, Poole, Dorset BH15 1LL, England
Distributed in Canada by Oak Tree Press Ltd.
% Canadian Manda Group, 215 Lakeshore Boulevard East
Toronto, Ontario M5A 3W9
Manufactured in the United States of America
All rights reserved
Library of Congress Catalog Card No.: 81-8764
Sterling ISBN 0-8069-5428-0 Trade
       ISBN 0-8069-5429-9 Library

Contents

Color sections following pages 16, 96, 112

To Pootchie
and to my daughter, Carolyn
—both living dolls

Acknowledgments

I wish to thank in particular Dorothy and Don Blankley for their kindness and consideration in allowing me so many visits to their home to photograph their dolls and discuss them. The majority of the dolls pictured here are from their collection.

I also wish to thank Caroline Greunke, Viktoria Richter, and Effie Colby for allowing me access to their dolls and for the use of their color slides of dolls.

I thank Pamela Brown of Sotheby Parke Bernet, Richard Withington, Auctions By Theriault, and Kim McKim of Kimport Dolls for their co-operative responses to my many questions.

Additional thanks to Irving Chais of the New York Doll Hospital for providing information on doll repair, to Flora Gill Jacobs of the Washington Dolls' House and Toy Museum for use of the 1907 L. H. Mace & Co. catalogue, and to Robby Rinaldi for his fine photography. I also wish to thank Hannah Reich of Sterling Publishing Company for the doll restoration photography and for securing tips on doll conservation.

Figure 1. Doll makers at work, and a kiln. Original woodcuts from the *Hortus Sanitatus, 1491.*

∽ 1 ∽

Introduction

Doll collecting today is one of the largest collecting phenomena in the country. Not only has interest in this fascinating area of antiques skyrocketed within the past few years; the prices of many dolls and doll accessories have skyrocketed also, necessitating upon the part of the advanced collector, as well as the novice enthusiast, extreme caution and certainly the utmost discrimination in establishing and expanding a collection. This is said neither to frighten away the newcomer to the field, nor to create a climate of pessimism among the experienced. Quality antiques have always commanded premium prices. In an inflated economy, escalated prices are a fact of life that must be considered objectively and dealt with prudently.

Escalated prices force collectors to proceed cautiously. Certainly in today's economy, none but the affluent can indulge in either indiscriminate or impulse buying. This situation encourages collectors to proceed as in fact they always should—taking time, care, and patience when shopping for that ever-intriguing and ever-elusive quarry, the next doll.

Indeed, it is for just such collectors that this book has been prepared. This book is neither a simple picture book, although there are many helpful illustrations, nor a price guide. It is not a detailed history of doll manufacture or an in-depth study of only one particular doll type or category. Rather, it is a common-sense guidebook to doll collecting, one that is intended to simplify the process of collecting by offering tips and guidelines for selecting dolls sensibly and knowledgeably, negotiating with doll dealers to the buyer's best possible advantage, and managing the growth of a collection to ensure the most pleasure along the way.

Many of the suggestions offered in this book are applicable to several areas of collecting. They are not limited to antique and collectible dolls. But it is to the doll collector that this book is specifically addressed.

Finally, I have this to say to the collector who can produce from a shelf that one exceptional Kewpie doll with a downcast face and double row of wings: Tell the world about it. You will be enriching doll history, and you will be the subject of praise among collectors for many years to come.

Figure 2. Just as today, advertisers one hundred years ago recognized the enormous sales potential of dolls. This paper-doll giveaway was used to bolster the sales of Hood's Pills.

2

Knowing Your ABC's

Whatever the method a collector may devise for purchasing dolls—and several shall be discussed in this book—the more informed a collector is, the better the collection will be. In this opening chapter are a series of questions designed to test the doll collector's expertise in today's rapidly changing market.

Some questions reflect long-accepted collecting habits while others point to the shifting attitudes and concepts in the current doll market. Consider that for every generalization, there is a collector or an authority somewhere who can legitimately disprove it. The late Genevieve Angione, lover of dolls and author of many books and articles about them, made the excellent point that there must always be a beginning in any subject.

Knowledge grows; it does not spring up whole suddenly. Every intellectual discipline and creative endeavor bears witness to this.

There are an infinite number of possibilities in any field. Contemporary researchers in the doll-collecting field are doing studies that reveal new facts about dolls. As the field expands, previously unpublicized or unknown information is brought to light.

Keep in mind that in this text, the term "antique" doll applies to dolls produced seventy-five years ago or earlier. The term "collectible" doll applies to dolls produced between twenty-five and seventy-five years ago. The terms *modern* and *contemporary* apply to dolls produced within the last twenty-five years. As informed collectors realize, there is a substantial overlapping of doll types and manufacturing techniques. Thus, the dates are for convenient referencing primarily, and the collector should remain both flexible and open-minded about them.

How would you answer these questions? A detailed discussion of each of these points follows this list.

A   Are *all dolls* worthy of acquisition?

B   Are *bisque-headed dolls* in greater demand than the more recent compositions and vinyls? Do bisques still command higher prices?

C   Are *closed-mouth dolls* more prized by collectors than open-mouth dolls?

D   Is *doll collecting* a relatively recent phenomenon?

E   Does *the eye type* affect the value of the doll?

F   Are *French dolls* more prized by collectors than any other type of dolls?

G   Are *German dolls* considered less desirable than French dolls?

H   Is the *head of a doll* its most important part?

I   Is the doll-making *industry* more innovative today than it was one hundred years ago?

J   Are *Jumeau* dolls among the most elite of all dolls?

K   Are *kid-bodied dolls* inferior to composition or to bisque-bodied dolls?

L   Are *large dolls* in greater demand than small dolls?

M   Do the *markings* on a doll offer a foolproof indication of its origin?

N   Are *name dolls* considered collector prizes?

O   Should *original clothing* on a doll be preserved, even if it is in poor condition?

P   Do early *photographs* of dolls have any historical or collector value?

Q   Is *quality* in a doll generally in the eye of the beholder?

R   Have *reproduction dolls* any place at all in a serious collection?

S   Is *segmentation* (jointing) in a doll of substantial interest or concern to collectors?

T   Can dolls serve as *teaching* devices?

U   Are *unmarked dolls* generally risky buys?

V   Do *values* of dolls change erratically?

W   Is it true that *wax dolls* make poor investments because they are so fragile?

X   Do "*X-tra*" *interests* usually evolve from an initial interest in dolls?

Y   Are *young people* becoming more actively involved in doll collecting than they were in times past?

Z   Can *zylonite* dolls be considered the first of the plastics?

Figure 3. Victorian advertising card for a doll dressmaker.

Are all dolls worthy of acquisition?

In the most general sense, they are and always have been. No single authority on the subject has either the right or the rank to dictate what does—or what does not—constitute a doll collection. While some collectors might be indifferent to any but the choicest of the French or German bisques, an ever-increasing collector population is now avidly pursuing the more recent dolls, the compositions of the 1930's and 1940's, the hard plastic dolls, the vinyls.

In part, of course, interest in these later dolls stems from their affordability. But financial circumstances do not always influence the collector's area of concentration or preference. I recall several years ago visiting the home of a Connecticut collector whose pride in a stairwell display of Barbie dolls seemed to equal her pride in some of the choicest French and German bisque dolls that I have ever seen. This is another way of saying that you should collect what you like, as well as what you can afford. Far too many novice collectors are easily swayed by "name" dolls, or by the particular type an established collector friend has already accumulated. You must be in charge of your own collection, and not let someone else's concept of a collection take charge of you.

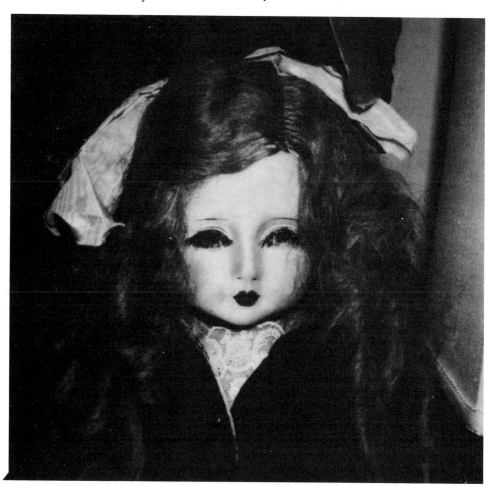

Figure 4. The "bee-stung" lips and the heavily lacquered lashes accentuate the 1920's flapper look of this Mary Pickford doll.

Are bisque-headed dolls in greater demand than the more recent compositions and vinyls? Do bisques still command higher prices?

Once again, circumstances alter cases. The bisque doll has commanded prime collector attention for many years, but as its price continues to climb, more and more collectors are concentrating on other doll types. Celebrity dolls from the 1930's and 1940's have widespread collector appeal today, particularly among American collectors, as do certain of the plastics and vinyls from more recent decades. Many such dolls now command the prices the bisques commanded only a few years back. As one indication of the law of supply and demand in the doll world, a 36-inch (91.4-cm) vinyl Shirley Temple sold for well over $1,000* at the time of this writing. Although there are many vinyl Shirleys available, all dating from the 1950's or later, so few were manufactured in this large size, and so great is the demand for them, that the prices they fetch surpass the prices on many of the earlier composition Shirleys. Some of the · same collectors who scoffed at the composition doll twenty-five years ago are scoffing at the vinyls today, but vinyl dolls are here to stay, and are certain to grow in collector appeal with the passage of time.

Are closed-mouth dolls more prized by collectors than open-mouth dolls?

As a rule, this is certainly so of the antique dolls, but there is an interesting paradox involved. Open-mouth dolls with ceramic teeth were a manufacturing innovation of the late-nineteenth century. While it is true that dolls with teeth composed of milk glass and such unusual substances as bamboo appeared far earlier in the century, the large-scale manufacture of dolls with single or double rows of gleaming pearly whites did not attain widespread production much before the end of the 1800's.

Figure 5. Thirty-three-inch (82.5-cm) German bisque-headed, kid-bodied doll.

Since response to the open-mouth dolls was overwhelmingly enthusiastic, doll makers produced them by the millions, despite the fact that inclusion of teeth was an added production cost. While the closed-mouth doll may not have been as costly to manufacture, fewer of them were ever produced; thus, closed-mouth dolls command premium prices today, simply because of their comparative scarcity.

As always when talking about dolls, however, there are few easy or pat explanations. While closed-mouth dolls are undeniably desirable, not every closed-mouth automatically surpasses in value its open-mouth cousin. An

* The few doll prices quoted in this book are the prices at which specific dolls sold at a particular place and time. The reader must not jump to the conclusion that every doll that seems similar is automatically of the same value. For a more detailed discussion of the circumstances affecting doll values, see chapter 4, "Establishing and Expanding a Collection."

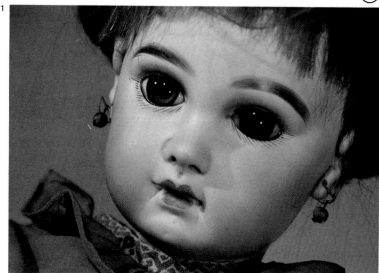

This close-up of a Jumeau head reveals the fine feathering of the lashes and brows and the luminous paperweight eyes prized by collectors of French dolls.

Many contemporary collectors are eclectic in their tastes. They acquire dolls of different types and from different eras. The Madame Alexander "Little Women" series is a perennial favorite, as are early lady dolls (*bottom right*) and peddler dolls (*bottom center*).

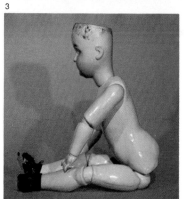

The undressed doll shows a typical German ball-jointed body. This type is currently growing in collector esteem.

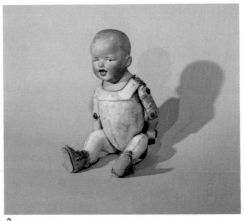

1

2

The wide variety of materials that manufacturers have used to create doll bodies often surprises the beginning collector. Note that the all-bisque (upper left) is realistically proportioned, in contrast to the kid-bodied baby next to it. The dolls featured below vary from the pleasingly out-of-proportion shoulder-head at left, to the well proportioned, wood-bodied lady doll to the right. Fine detailing of the hands contrasts sharply with the crudeness of the legs and torso on the cloth-bodied china-head doll at the center.

3

4

5

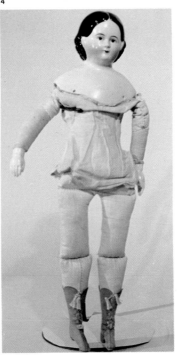

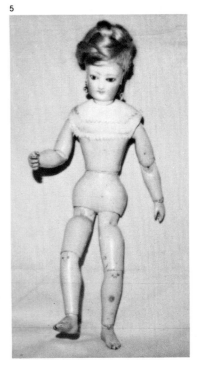

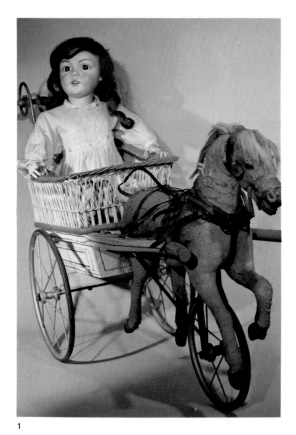

1

2

An appealing prop can heighten the interest of an otherwise ordinary doll. With the exception of the Oriental (bottom left), all of the doll types pictured are readily accessible on today's market. Their accessories make all the difference.

3

4

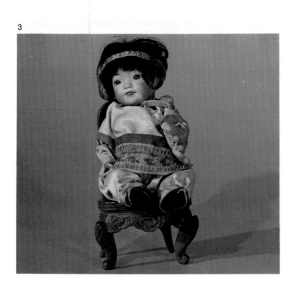

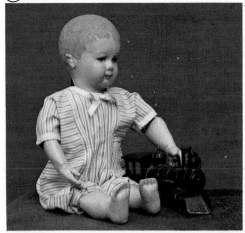

Baby dolls have always been of interest to collectors. The examples on this page illustrate the ingenuity of doll manufacturers in capturing facial expressions that are both appealing and realistic. All dolls were referred to as "babies" until the beginning of the nineteenth century. However, it was not until the beginning of the twentieth century that dolls whose bodies, as well as faces, closely resembled those of real babies gained widespread popularity.

Figure 6. This closed-mouth French beauty goes by the initials "A.T.," for A. Thuillier.

open-mouth German of the so-called "dolly" type produced by Armand Marseille and several other companies will consistently sell for less than almost any closed-mouth German or French doll. But open-mouth dolls of French manufacture, including those produced by such firms as Steiner, Jumeau, and Bru, are worth far more than all but the most exceptional closed-mouth German.

Similarly, an open-mouth doll of either French or German origin will command a higher price than many closed-mouth examples if the particular doll in question is in some way unusual. An unusual doll might be one of mechanical construction, one that represents a seldom-seen variation of a doll of standard manufacture, or one that was in production so briefly that it has become a comparative rarity. Again, many factors must be taken into consideration when determining doll value.

As collectors of modern dolls can attest, there is currently no significant relationship between the mouth formation and the market price of modern dolls.

Is doll collecting a relatively recent phenomenon?

The answer to this question depends on what is meant by a collection. For as long as anyone can remember, or history books can record, little girls have treasured their dolls and collected them and cared for them. Among the relics found in ancient tombs, stone or terra cotta figures appear; the construction of these suggests that they were indeed intended as playthings rather than as religious artifacts. However, with the exception of adult interest in dollhouses or "baby" houses and cabinets three and four centuries ago, doll collecting by adult enthusiasts did not gain significant momentum until the early portion of the twentieth century.

This is also true of adult interest in related antique playthings, such as boys' cast-iron trains, trolleys, and cars. Real collector interest began to mount in the late 1930's and has accelerated rapidly ever since. Every state

Figure 7. This crèche doll is several hundred years old and came from a Spanish church.

has its network of doll clubs and federations, and magazines and newsletters keep collectors informed of the locations of doll shows and auctions.

Does the eye type affect the value of the doll?

There are several matters to be considered here. One consideration brings to mind the ever-popular Rose O'Neill Kewpie doll, which was generally produced with painted eyes, rather than inset glass ones. The few Kewpies that were produced with glass eyes are now priced many times higher than those with the more commonly available painted eyes.

What the collector must note and be ever alert to is whether or not the eye type is correct for the particular doll. If, at the time of manufacture, a doll had luminous "paperweight" eyes appropriate to earlier French dolls, and these eyes were later replaced with so-called "sleep" eyes, the value of that doll is adversely affected. In general, paperweight eyes elevate the value of a doll.

Another dramatic example of how eye type affects value is in the realm of the roguish, or "googly" glass eyes, the large, wafer-shaped eyes which glance to the side and which attained special popularity in the early years of the present century. A German doll with googly eyes may, as in the case of certain of the Kestners, bear a price tag in the thousands, whereas another doll by the same manufacturer with stationary or sleep eyes may be very moderately priced. Again, this reflects the law of supply and demand, as well as collector caprice. Googly-eyed dolls are very popular in today's market.

While there are subtle distinctions in eye type, color, shape, and manner of insertion in modern and collectible dolls, such distinctions do not yet have either as definite or widespread a bearing upon the market price as they do with antique dolls.

Figure 8. S.F.B.J. character doll with open mouth and blue-grey stationary eyes.

Figure 9. The expressive Bru (left) and the long-faced Jumeau represent, for many, two of the most beautiful dolls ever produced. On today's market, they are also among the most expensive.

Are French dolls more prized by collectors than any other doll types?

That they are has always been a truism in the doll world—and not without considerable justification. The finest French dolls, those produced during the golden years of manufacture (1860–1890), are conspicuous for the fine quality of the bisque, the glow to the eyes, the extraordinary delicacy with which the mouth, lashes, and brows have been hand painted.

What present-day collectors must recognize, however, is that the Germans also produced dolls of considerable beauty, despite the stereotyped impression which certain examples, such as the Armand Marseille 390, have in the past conveyed. Companies such as Kestner and Kammer & Reinhardt manufactured dolls as delightful and as meritorious as the French. In fact, some of the Kestner character babies and the beautiful Kestner Gibson girl hold their own with almost any of the French, as do many of the Kammer & Reinhardt dolls produced during the early years of the twentieth century.

Are German dolls less desirable than French dolls?

This question may seem redundant, in view of the preceding one. Nevertheless, as I have already stated, there are many fine German dolls equal in beauty and charm to their

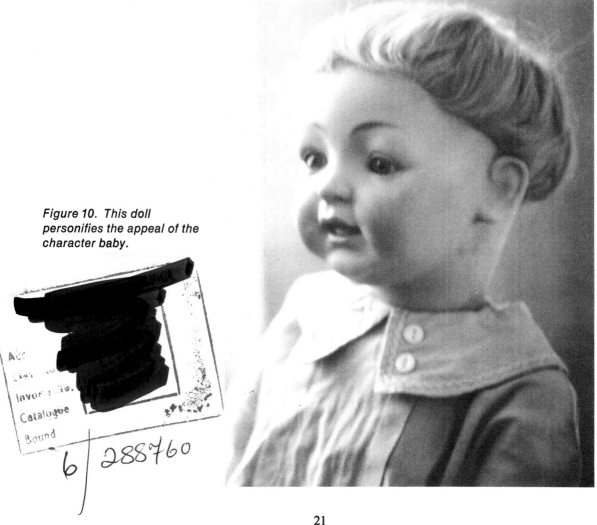

Figure 10. This doll personifies the appeal of the character baby.

French doll cousins. I know of several collectors, for whom money is little object, whose area of specialization is the German character babies from the 1910–1920's era. Such dolls have great appeal. Accordingly, prices have been climbing. Gebruder Heubach is one of the German manufacturers whose expressive bisque-headed character dolls have attracted widespread collector attention. The much-respected Kestner firm is another. A collector could easily spend a lifetime seeking out the character types from these two firms alone.

Some excellent reproduction German doll bodies are now on the market. There is nothing wrong with acquiring a reproduction doll or doll body, and reasons for doing so are discussed on pages 35–36. The collector should of course be aware that the item is not an original, and the doll or the doll body should be priced accordingly. Of particular importance here is the fact that there is a limited, but active, market for reproduction German dolls. This bears witness to the desirability of the originals.

Is the head of a doll its most important part?

No matter how times and trends create changes in the world of doll collecting, the head itself will always define the doll. Even a hundred years ago, when dolls were manufactured as children's playthings, and little or no thought was given to their becoming antiques or collectibles, the major focus was generally the head.

Indeed, in many factories the same artisans sat year after year at the same tables, delicately hand painting such facial features as lashes and brows with a skill and a speed that were a wonder to behold. Those owl-like brows that almost meet at the nose, giving to the French Jumeau doll its characteristic and eminently distinguishable look, were hand-applied by masters of their craft.

While the Kestner firm in Germany did resort to the use of a stencil as a cost-saving device for the application of mouth paint on certain of their dolls, most doll manufacturers relied completely upon creative handwork for the completion of facial features, for setting in

Figure 11. Doll heads on display at the New York Doll Hospital.

the luminous paperweight eyes, and for implanting human hair on the finest and most lustrous of the doll wigs.

A curiosity of early doll manufacture, at least from the standpoint of the modern-day collector, is that similar attention was seldom lavished on doll bodies, which frequently seem both crude and clumsy in contrast to their heads. One notable exception to this was the mechanical doll, whose intricate and delicate mechanisms were incorporated into the body structure. Also exceptional are the rarer French lady doll bodies, which both in manner of composition and degree of articulation are such works of art that current owners often display these dolls unclothed.

Is the doll-making industry more innovative today than it was one hundred years ago?

Although the modern parent can buy dolls that wave, walk, talk, drink, and sport elaborate wardrobes and hairdos, the assumption that any of the current dolls represent radical departures from the past is erroneous. Competition among the leading European doll manufacturers reached a veritable fever-pitch one hundred years ago, this situation partly attributable to the then newfound knowledge that mass advertising paid off handsomely.

Each year—the decade beginning with 1880 presenting several notable examples—manufacturers attempted to outdo one another in their bid for foreign and domestic sales. They promoted their latest doll creations at widely attended international exhibitions, exhibitions at which they competed for medals and prizes and also at which they whetted the buying appetite of the public at large. Dolls on display at such exhibits were frequently dressed by skilled couturiers in the latest fashions. In their zeal for exclusivity, firms such as Jumeau went so far as to include on their doll box-lids warnings against the hazards of a compromise purchase. "Accept no substitutes," and "Beware of imitations," were standard admonishments to prospective doll "mothers."

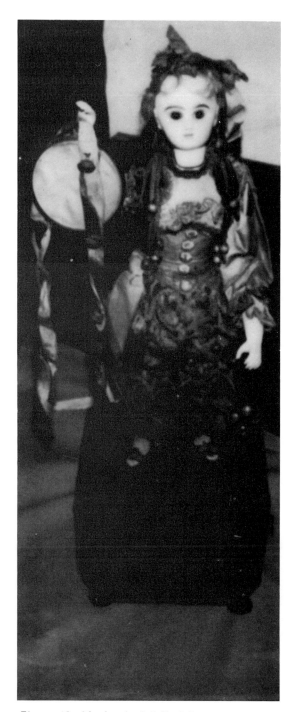

Figure 12. Mechanical doll of Jumeau manufacture.

23

It is in this very climate of competition that multi-faced dolls and dolls that could cry or talk by means of voice mechanisms and pull-strings reached their zenith of popularity. By 1879, Bru had patented a nursing doll (*bébé têteur*) with a bulb in the head for absorbing fluids. This was followed by an intriguing, though far less commercially successful "eating" doll (*bébé gourmand*) and, in the 1890's, by a doll with an expandable chest.

Throughout the latter part of the nineteenth century, such manufacturers as Bru and Jumeau continued experimentations with body materials, with techniques for the jointing of doll limbs and the attachment of doll heads, as well as with eye mechanisms. These firms, and others in France and Germany, worked on an independent basis, although they sometimes also worked in cooperation with one another in order to perfect a particular patent design, or to supply the unending need for parts. The Kestner firm in Germany, for example, manufactured many of the doll heads for Jumeau during a certain period in Jumeau's production. Simon & Halbig, another German doll maker, was also a large exporter and supplier of doll heads.

Although the mechanical doll was by no means exclusive to Jumeau, to Steiner, or even to French manufacture, these two companies were responsible for some of the most exquisite nineteenth-century examples. "Mechanicals," as they are generally dubbed by collectors, are the dolls which, when set in motion by means of a windup key or similar device, execute graceful dance steps, raise and lower boxes, mirrors, and bird cages, play musical instruments, rock babies, or even breathe by means of mechanisms which cause the chest of the doll to heave visibly.

In fairness to contemporary doll manufacturers, the cost of labor and materials alone would prohibit large-scale production of dolls such as these for today's market. The point is, however, that aside from evolutionary changes in the raw materials used to manufacture doll parts—the change from bisque to composition, for example, or from composition to plastic and vinyl—there is little in current doll pro-

duction that had not been anticipated well over a century ago.

Are Jumeau dolls among the most elite of all dolls?

Undeniably, the Jumeau doll ranks high on the list of those dolls most coveted by collectors. The recent Jumeau doll craze (no other word more adequately describes the phenomenon) sent prices spiralling well into the four-figure range just a few years ago, underscoring not only the doll's tremendous popularity but also its particular mystique.

Some dolls may be rarer than the Jumeaux—certain Brus or A.T.'s (A. Thuillier), for ex-

Figure 13. A truly choice Jumeau with flawless bisque and earlier style unjointed wrists.

24

ample. Other dolls may be more glamorous than the Jumeau, with its tendency toward a heavy-browed, owlish look. Still other dolls may surpass the Jumeau in body quality, or in the detailing of hands, or in the structuring of the feet. But certainly no doll has been more widely discussed, desired or dreamed about by collectors, or more vigorously promoted by its manufacturer during a production period which spanned well over one hundred years, from the 1840's to the 1950's. That this doll company was turning out almost a quarter of a million completed dolls per year by 1884 offers some suggestion as to the total volume of Jumeaux which reached the market place. For all their one-time abundance, however, the chances today of finding a perfectly preserved example in all-original, factory condition are, at best, remote. The finest-quality Jumeaux are being snapped up by dealers, by collectors, and by doll museums as quickly as they become available on the market. Cost seems to be little or no impediment. True, the experienced collector may justify "for investment purposes" an expenditure of well over $3,000 for a Jumeau that in 1970 might have cost a mere $300. Yet such is the appeal of the Jumeau doll that talk about investment potential is often just a thinly guised pretense for plain and simple love of the doll. "Considering what I just spent on her," a collector friend recently confided, "I know I should place her in a vault." Then, brushing a tiny fleck of dust from the doll's wig, she shrugged and added, "But I can't. I just can't put her in a box and hide her away somewhere."

It is the eyes which create the mystique. Jumeau paperweight eyes can be pensive or soulful, slightly smiling or slightly sad. Occasionally, the eyes truly seem to follow you as you approach the displayed doll or walk around her. This may not seem so remarkable when one considers that Jumeau hand selected and then, over a period of years, carefully trained the women who actually did the glass blowing for these eyes.

Of all the Jumeaux ever produced, the "long-faced" Jumeau is the example most generally regarded by collectors as the manufacturer's production triumph. A $10,000 price tag is no longer unusual, and even this figure is destined to rise.

One more point is essential here. Collectors, especially beginning collectors, hear so much about the Jumeau and the Bru French doll that there is sometimes the impression that these two firms, and only one or two others, were responsible for all high-quality French dolls ever produced. This is simply not the case. Many firms produced fine dolls in France during the latter part of the nineteenth century. These include Rabery and Delphieu, E. Denamur, Fleischman and Blodel, and Fernand Gaultier. French doll production continued into the twentieth century, although the efforts to stem the tide of German competition resulted in a gradual lowering of production costs and, in some instances, production standards.

The final Jumeau dolls are from 1953. Unfortunately, they but dimly suggest the aura and the excitement of the firm's earlier and more representative dolls.

Are kid-bodied dolls inferior to composition or to bisque-bodied dolls?

Since just about every substance imaginable has been used at one time or another in the manufacture of doll bodies, any pat assumption as to the inferiority or superiority of one type over another must yield to a variety of considerations: inferior or superior how, to what, and why. There is a valid point to such questions. Experience has shown that many collectors, when evaluating dolls for purchase, are unduly influenced by current trends in collecting, or are ignorant or misinformed. While it is true that not every doll collector has either the interest or the time and patience to do in-depth research on doll history and manufacture, simply by preserving relics of the past every collector in a very real sense is both a curator and a historian. Certainly collectors should have basic, even if minimal, knowledge of the substances used at various times in the production of the dolls they are currently collecting.

It is invalid to assume, as one national dealer

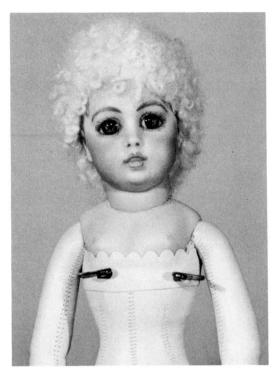

Figure 14. Kid-bodied Bru (bébé teteur) as interpreted by contemporary doll artist Marianne DeNunez.

once assured me I must, that the bisque-headed, kid-bodied doll is "low man" on the collector totem pole. While it is true that many cheaply produced, coarse-complexioned dolls of inferior quality are, indeed, kid-bodied dolls, it is also true that countless dolls of poor quality are composition or bisque-bodied. Conversely, the finest French kid bodies were made of soft and supple skins and were completely hand-sewn. True, the articulation on kid-bodied dolls was often clumsy. Eventual settling of the body contents, which ranged from saw-dust to horsehair, often resulted in ungainly postures. Nevertheless, some very beautiful dolls were manufactured with kid bodies. Among these are the French lady dolls of the 1860's and 1870's, considered so beautiful by many that they collect these dolls to the exclusion of all others. Kid-bodied Brus, especially those manufactured during the 1880's, have always been accorded enthusiastic collector favor.

Still, all things being equal, prevailing collector trends are such that the composition, jointed version of a doll also produced in a kid-bodied version will often fetch the higher price on today's market. One has only to examine comparative figures in the leading doll price guides and auction catalogues to affirm this fact. Some collectors still favor kid-bodied dolls, citing the ease with which such dolls lend themselves to costuming. Others opt for a kid-bodied doll whenever it becomes evident that the doll's production in kid took place over a limited period of time only, rendering that particular doll a comparative rarity. Until quite recently, and primarily as a simple matter of preference, European collectors were willing to pay twice as much as American collectors for some kid-bodied dolls.

Whether the doll of the moment is a ball-jointed French *bébé* or a vinyl Shirley, the canny collector is the one who combines knowledge of dolls and of doll-collecting trends with personal preferences and convictions. One doll type is not automatically inferior—or superior—to a different type.

Are large dolls in greater demand than small dolls?

By "large dolls" collectors most commonly mean dolls that are 32 inches (81.3 cm) and taller. Such dolls have become extremely popular in recent years, with prices climbing well into the four-figure range for the choicest examples. The high price currently commanded by the 36-inch (91.4-cm) vinyl Shirley Temple has already been noted (p. 16). While interest in size has not quite matched interest in type (the recent run on Jumeaux, for example, as well as on other choice French and German bisques), the demand for large dolls is sufficient to raise the obvious question: Why?

I believe there are at least two significant reasons. Large dolls—some approaching a life-like size of 42 inches (1.1 m)—present a striking appearance. When placed in a hearthside rocking chair or when propped upright on a bed, alone or cradling an early toy, a book, or even a smaller doll, the large doll lends dramatic visual focus to a collection. In addition, the collector who does not wish to pay the price the choicest smaller dolls presently command may take great pleasure in the acquisition of a doll whose appearance adds zest to a collection without depleting the treasury. While it is still possible to obtain some examples of the larger dolls in the moderate price ranges, truly choice small dolls, with the exception of some compositions and vinyls, are no longer available at moderate prices.

Increase in the size of a doll does not necessarily mean increase in the beauty of a doll,

however. While dolls such as the Simon & Halbig 1079 retain a limpid beauty in the life-sized editions, others do not. I have seen some grotesque examples: large dolls with vacant, expressionless faces and crude facial detailing. Sometimes these defects are not as obvious in smaller versions of the same doll. They may also be the result of poor-quality workmanship.

To say that large dolls are in greater demand than small dolls, then, is to miss the point. Some are. Some are not. Once again, much depends upon the merits of the particular dolls under discussion.

Do the markings on a doll offer a foolproof indication of its origin?

If this were indeed the case, a great deal of confusion concerning the actual origins of certain dolls could be avoided. Markings on dolls refer to letters, numbers, and symbols stamped, embossed, or incised on the back of the doll's head, generally beneath the wig, and also on the shoulder plates. Markings may also be found on doll torsos and even on the bottom of the feet.

In mechanical dolls, the collector will often find the manufacturer's mark on the key-wind mechanism implanted within the doll's chest cavity, or on the key itself. Joseph Kallus, one of the most prolific and talented twentieth-century doll makers, used paper stickers with his name on them for most of his earlier dolls. For his later dolls (especially his vinyls), he often used his initials only, putting them at or behind the ears. Mattel Toys, which began doll production in the late 1940's, marks most of its dolls on the hips.

Markings may be an indication of the factory mould number, the style number, or the country or company of manufacture. Some doll markings are detailed and extensive and incorporate elaborate motifs, as is the case with certain Kestners and Steiners. Other doll markings are cryptic to the point of obscurity.

Figure 15. A large German doll with clear, well-defined features. She has her original human-hair wig.

Manufacturers differed as to the types of markings and marking codes they employed, but since they worked independently, it is not uncommon to find that rival companies sometimes unwittingly used identical style numbers as designations for two decidedly different dolls.

Problems in identification are compounded by the fact that some companies used paper labels, which are susceptible to damage and loss, or did not mark their dolls at all. In the latter case, this may have been for any of several reasons. The Jumeau firm, for example, carefully avoided stamping its famous factory name on dolls of particular degrees of imperfection. Such dolls could then be sold at reduced prices without tarnishing the company image.

Had early doll manufacturers considered the interests of present-day collectors, they undoubtedly would have been more precise than they were in their codings. Since dolls were initially intended as playthings only, documentation was largely for the convenience of factory assemblage and occasionally for advertising a particular doll or doll company.

There are some excellent guide books available for collectors who wish to authenticate a doll's origins by means of its markings. The authors of such books consistently point out the difficulties and problems of this method; nevertheless, familiarity with such texts is highly recommended.

Figure 16. The graphite shading shows off this incised marking. The term "deposé" was used by the French as an indication of the doll's registration.

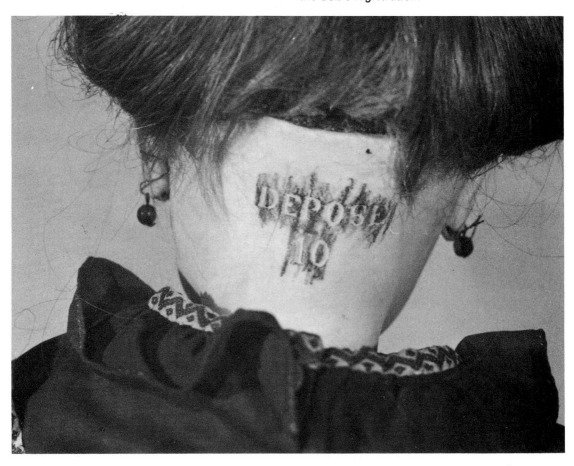

Are name dolls considered collector prizes?

A good way of answering this would be to say that *some* name dolls are indeed very much prized. The appearance of a name somewhere on the doll, or even attached by means of a sticker or a tag to the doll or to the doll's clothing, elevates the value of the doll over an identical, but unidentified, example.

The appearance of the name alone, however, does not automatically boost the collector appeal of every doll, no matter how ordinary. Collectors are not rushing to buy the tin-headed dolls marked "Minerva" or the "Pet Name" common-head chinas of the early 1900's. The poor quality of most of these dolls, as well as their sheer abundance, makes their rise in value unlikely—at least for now.

When speaking of name dolls, incidentally, the contemporary collector should be aware that old-time collectors tended to assign names to particular dolls or doll types. Thus, the term "covered wagon" refers to chinas of the 1850's era, so-named because in dress, and most particularly in hair style, they resemble the hardy pioneer women of the American Frontier.

Another popular china type from the 1860's is referred to as a "Civil War" china. Again, this is a collector-assigned name, used to distinguish one doll from another within particular, recognized doll categories. It is not a name assigned to a doll at the time of manufacture. The collector contemplating the purchase of a "covered wagon" or "Civil War" type, then, should be influenced more by the merits of the particular doll than by its nickname.

If by name dolls one includes personality or celebrity dolls of the 1930's and later, they take on still greater significance. Among the manufacturers of dolls more recent than bisques and chinas, no manufacturer in this country has produced more outstanding name dolls than Madame Alexander. Her Dionne Quintuplets, Jane Withers, Sonja Henie and Margaret O'Brien, as well as many others, have become enormously popular among collectors. Many of the early Alexanders were made of composition and then, as in the case of the "Little Women" series, were carried over into hard-plastic production. Many Alexander dolls have the manufacturer's name, as well as the doll's name, both on clothing labels and on identifying tags, these sometimes pinned to the clothing or suspended by a string from the doll's wrist.

Absence of such tags and labels undermines considerably the collector value of the more recent dolls. Thus, a Sonja Henie or a Dionne Quintuplet look-alike does not find as ready a market as does the properly tagged version of either doll.

In contemplating the purchase of a name doll of any era, the questions a collector must consider are these: Who assigned the name? When and how was the name assigned? Does proof-of-name alone warrant purchasing?

Figure 17. Even pins for Shirley Temple dolls are being reproduced for today's market. The one on this Shirley is an original.

Should original clothing on a doll be preserved, even if it is in poor condition?

Clothing original to a doll includes the clothing which came with the doll at the time of manufacture. It also includes clothing made for the doll while it belonged to its first owner. Thus, a doll with factory-original clothing and either factory accessories or clothing and accessories made for the doll by an older sister, a mother, or a loving aunt should all be considered original.

Experienced collectors are well aware that many dolls, including some of the finest French and German bisques, came from the factory dressed only in simple chemises. Sometimes also, the outer garments original to the doll were attractive enough to tempt the adult buyer, but so flimsy that they surely could not have survived for long in the hands of their young owners. Many factory-made outfits resembled the buildings in boom towns of America's Wild West era. They had hastily constructed, gaudily decorated fronts, but very little substantial material or fastening to hold them together, and no fabric at the back.

Turn-of-the-century catalogues of the sort produced by Sears Roebuck & Co. repeatedly advertised doll outfits and accessories in assorted sizes, to supplement the meager garments original to many dolls. In 1903, for example, Sears Roebuck sold a five-piece colored lawn outfit, consisting of a dress and a hat trimmed with lace, white lawn bloomers, and a skirt and corset trimmed with Valenciennes lace. A customer could buy this outfit for $2.00 for dolls 15 to 21 inches (38.1 cm to 53.3 cm) high, and $2.45 for dolls 24 to 27 inches (61 cm to 68.6 cm) high. The same catalogue listed such items as capes and muffs, sweaters and hats—even a doll's golf vest knit from Shetland floss, at a price of just twenty-five cents.

In keeping with the definition of what constitutes original doll clothing, any catalogue-

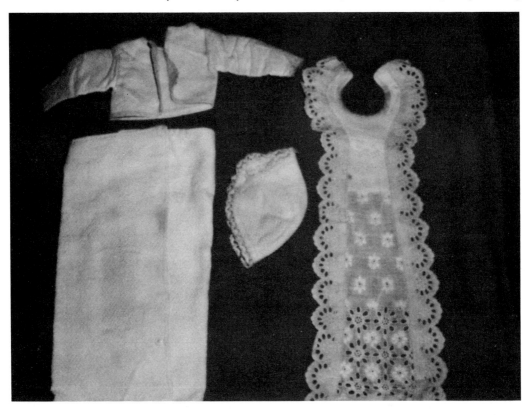

Figure 18. These wardrobe accessories came with a nineteenth-century Steiner doll.

30

DOLLS—Continued.

METAL DOLL HEADS.

An entirely New Line. Appearance and Finish is positively superior to any line now on the market.

Painted Eyes and Painted Hair.

No.		Per Doz.
804/00	1¾ in. across shoulders.	$0.85
1	2¼ in. across shoulders.	1.25
2	2⅜ in. across shoulders.	1.50
3	2½ in. across shoulders.	1.75
4	2⅞ in. across shoulders.	2.00
5	3⅜ in. across shoulders.	2.75
6	3⅝ in. across shoulders.	3.25
7	4 in. across shoulders.	3.75
8	4⅜ in. across shoulders.	4.25
9	4⅞ in. across shoulders.	5.50

METAL DOLL HEADS.

Painted Hair and Glass Eyes.

No.		Per Doz.
804/22	2⅜ in. across shoulders.	$1.75
23	2½ in. across shoulders.	2.00
24	3 in. across shoulders.	2.75
25	3⅜ in. across shoulders.	3.25
26	3⅝ in. across shoulders.	3.75
27	4 in. across shoulders.	4.00
28	4⅜ in. across shoulders.	4.50
29	4¾ in. across shoulders.	5.50

METAL DOLL HEADS.
Painted Eyes and Flowing Hair.

No.		Per Doz.
804/31	2½ in. across shoulders.	$2.00
32	3 in. across shoulders.	2.75
33	3⅛ in. across shoulders.	3.75
34	3⅜ in. across shoulders.	4.25

METAL DOLL HEADS.

Moving Eyes and Good Quality Wig.

No.		Per Doz.
804/41	2½ in. across shoulders.	$3.75
42	2⅞ in. across shoulders.	4.25
43	3⅛ in. across shoulders.	5.50
44	3¼ in. across shoulders.	6.50
45	3½ in. across shoulders.	7.50
46	3⅞ in. across shoulders.	8.00

CELLULOID DOLLS' HEADS.
Painted Hair and Painted Eyes.

No.		Per Doz.
J 7½	2⅛ in. across shoulders..	$0.80
9	2½ in. across shoulders..	1.25
10	3 in. across shoulders..	1.75
11	3⅛ in. across shoulders..	2.00
12	3½ in. across shoulders..	2.50
14	4 in. across shoulders..	3.50
15	4½ in. across shoulders..	4.00
16½	5 in. across shoulders..	5.50

CELLULOID DOLLS' HEADS.

Steady Glass Eyes, Good Quality Curly Wig.

No.		Per Doz.
K/8½	2½ in. across shoulders..	$2.00
10	3 in. across shoulders..	3.25
11	3¼ in. across shoulders..	3.75
12	3⅜ in. across shoulders..	4.25
14	4 in. across shoulders..	6.50
15	4½ in. across shoulders..	7.50
16½	5 in. across shoulders..	8.50

56

Figure 19. Pages like these from the 1907 L. H. Mace & Co. catalogue are prized by collectors. (Used by permission of the Washington Dolls' House and Toy Museum.)

DOLLS—Continued.

RUBBER DOLL HEADS.

Painted Hair and Painted Eyes.

No.		Per Doz.
2100/40	2¾ in. across shoulders.	$2.00
41	3 in. across shoulders.	3.25
42	3¼ in. across shoulders.	3.75
43	3½ in. across shoulders.	4.25

SOCKET DOLLS' HEADS.

Bisque, with Moving Eyes.

No.		Per Doz.
406/174	2¾ inches high	$1.50
175	2⅞ inches high	1.75
176	3 inches high	2.00
177	3⅛ inches high	3.25
178	3½ inches high	3.50
179	3¾ inches high	4.00
180	4 inches high	4.25
181	4½ inches high	4.50
182	4¾ inches high	5.00
183	5 inches high	5.50
184	5¼ inches high	6.00
185	6 inches high	7.50
186	6¼ inches high	8.50
187	7 inches high	10.50
188	7½ inches high	12.00

BISQUE SOCKET DOLLS' HEADS.

With Curly Wigs attached, Moving Eyes.

No.		Per Doz.
1111/1	3½ inches high	$2.25
2	3¾ inches high	2.50
3	4 inches high	3.00
4	4½ inches high	3.50
5	4¾ inches high	4.00
6	5 inches high	4.50
7	5¼ inches high	5.00
8	5½ inches high	6.00
9	6 inches high	6.50
10	6¼ inches high	7.50
11	6¾ inches high	8.50

BISQUE BABIES.

Jointed Arms and Legs, Glass Eyes, Curly Hair.

No.		Per Doz.
1203/7	3½ inches long	$0.40
8	4 inches long	.45
9	5 inches long	.71
11	6 inches long	.80

As Above, with Moving Eyes.

No.		Per Doz.
1203/11	5 inches long	$0.85
12	6 inches long	1.25

Better Quality Bisque Babies, Jointed Arms and Legs, Painted Eyes, Long Hair.

No.		Per Doz.
1101/9	3¼ inches long	$0.40
10	5 inches long	.75
11	5½ inches long	.85

As Above, with Moving Eyes.

No.		Per Doz.
1101/0	6½ inches long	$1.75
2	7 inches long	2.00

As Above, Moving Eyes, Sewed Wig, Each in a Box.

No.		Per Doz.
1101/3	5¾ inches long	$2.00
4	6¾ inches long	3.25
5	7¼ inches long	3.75
6	8 inches long	4.25

Jointed Arms and Legs, Turning Head, Moving Eyes, Flowing Hair.

No.		Per Doz.
1101/7	5¾ inches long	$1.75
8	6½ inches long	2.00

NEGRO BABIES.

Jointed Arms and Legs, Black Woolly Hair, Painted Eyes. Boys and Girls, Assorted.

No.		Per Doz.
1203/21	4 inches long	$0.40
22	4½ inches long	.71
14	5½ inches long	.85

57

Figure 20. The L. H. Mace catalogue is discussed on page 74.

ordered doll clothing, purchased for the doll's first owner and chronologically and stylistically correct for the doll, may also be considered original.

Since documenting early doll clothes is often nearly impossible, collectors have taken to applying such terms as "as found" to early clothing which seems right for the doll but which cannot be positively authenticated.

The collector who is fortunate enough to obtain a doll with authentic original clothing should, as a matter of record, retain that clothing, no matter how tattered or frayed it has become. The collector who finds the original clothing an eyesore should have the original outfit copied as meticulously as possible, using materials and techniques from the period of the doll's manufacture. To update an early doll by replacing an original silk or wool outfit with a currently styled outfit in a synthetic fibre is a mistake. A doll so re-dressed may seem neat and clean and even more fashionable, unlike the frayed, orphanlike creature she may have appeared to be upon acquisition. Still, to re-dress a doll with today's fabrics and today's fashions is to distort social history and potentially to confuse the next generation of doll collectors. This commentary is as applicable to the multi-costumed Barbie doll from 1959 and later as it is to dolls from a much earlier era.

As the Colemans have pointed out in *The Collector's Book of Dolls' Clothes* (Crown Publishers, Inc., New York, 1975) a doll in its original dress is truly a three-dimensional model, reflecting economic as well as social history. How did fashionable ladies really dress? Possibly even more important, how did ordinary people dress, people whose style of clothing seldom appeared in fashion magazines and whose outfits—except for occasional bridal or christening gowns—were rarely preserved as family keepsakes? In many cases, the antique or collectible doll in its original clothing is the most reliable guide for answering these questions. Indeed, there are cases where the clothes a doll is wearing are of greater significance than the doll itself.

Do early photographs of dolls have any historical or collector value?

While it is true that early photographs of dolls have some value, *recent* photographs of dolls, when taken by a collector for the express purpose of recording data concerning a doll presumably now a part of a collection, have the greater value.

It is tempting and even commendable for collectors to acquire nostalgic and still relatively inexpensive photos of nineteenth-century children clutching a beloved doll. Flea markets and antiques shows abound with such little prizes, and little prizes they may be, in their own right. There, slightly faded but still plain to see, is the pencil-scrawled inscription on the back of an old sepia print: "Great Aunt Edna with dolly, 1893."

Even if the doll shows up clearly in the photograph, however, it is impossible to tell much conclusively from the two-dimensional, relatively toneless print. What, for example, were the colors in the doll's outfit? Was the garment on the doll homemade, professionally made by a seamstress, or commercially made at a factory? How was the doll's clothing constructed? What type of stitching was used? What width were the clothing panels? What types of closures were used? Equally important, of what nature, color, and quality were the doll's wig, eyes, head, and body? Were any of the original parts ever replaced? Added to these unknowns is the potential unreliability of the photograph and of its inscription. Who can be certain when and by whom the inscription was actually written? Is the date authentic? Was the doll pictured truly Aunt Edna's, or was it just a doll supplied by a professional studio to placate a child on picture-taking day?

Making accurate assessments about dolls on the basis of such photographs is, therefore, at best a risky proposition. As mementos, as general reminders of what people and dolls actually wore, as opposed to idealizations of style featured in such nineteenth-century fashion magazines as *Godey's* and *Peterson's*, they do have merit.

Is quality in a doll generally in the eye of the beholder?

Certainly in many cases this is so. There are dolls almost every collector would agree to be inferior examples. There are dolls whose body coloring is blotchy or uneven, dolls whose facial detailing lacks definition, dolls from all periods of time whose parts seem strangely out of proportion. In the case of homemade dolls, or factory-made dolls with homemade bodies, it may be that these very imperfections create appeal in the doll and therefore enhance the doll's desirability. In the case of factory-made dolls, however, such imperfections often result from poor-quality manufacturing, due to hasty or indifferent workmanship.

Still, there is a collector for virtually every doll ever produced, and some collectors actually do find beauty in dolls that many other collectors would consider inferior. *Quality, beauty,* and *desirability* are concepts which involve aesthetic awareness and appreciation. No matter how diligently doll experts may delineate standards of judgment, considerable license must always be granted for individual tastes and preferences.

Figure 21. A German, papier mâché hand puppet with inset glass eyes.

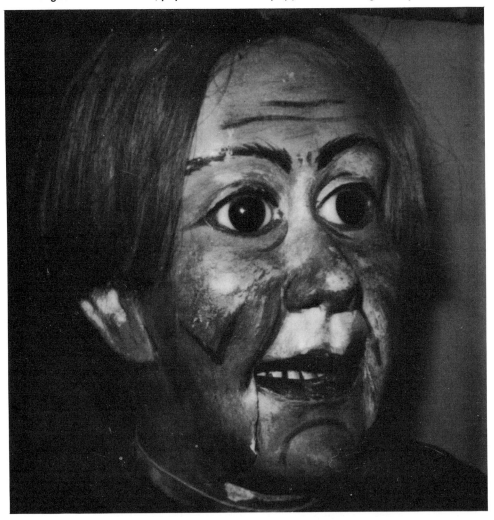

Have reproduction dolls any place at all in a serious collection?

This is a debatable matter. For the collector who covets a French Bru and yet cannot afford an original, acquisition of one of the fine reproduction Brus may be the most sensible compromise. Certainly any collector would be justifiably proud to own the exquisite reproduction Bru illustrated on this page. It was made by well-known doll artist Marianne DeNunez. The workmanship, including delicate hand stitching on the kid, is superb.

What is important to keep in mind is that placing a reproduction doll in among a collection of original dolls is a poor idea. The reproduction should stand alone or as part of a grouping of reproductions. In this way it attains merit, without implying that the collector is attempting a deception of any sort. On the subject of deception, it is important for the collector to be on guard, and not be taken in by the offer of a fine antique doll at a ridiculously low price. Nobody who knows the business is selling early dolls at bargain-basement prices these days. Chances are, the proferred doll is actually a reproduction.

Fortunately for the collector, reproduction dolls are usually easy to spot, because they often seem *too* good. The bisque, for example, may be satiny smooth, lacking the imperceptibly granular texture of the antique bisque. The surface, as a result of superior modern manufacturing techniques, is often flawless. Close examination of even the finest early bisque or china will reveal some degree of surface flecking. Experienced collectors look for such "flaws," when examining dolls, and are reassured by them.

As the price of antique dolls continues to climb, however, the challenge to reproduce

Figure 22. Oriental reproduction Bru.

35

them with foolproof exactitude becomes irresistible to some doll artists. The fact that cloth or kid surfaces look old or worn is no longer an assurance of authenticity. An occasional reproduction has even turned up with age cracks or outright breaks—these intended to diminish the suspicions of the unwary buyer. Conceivably, a doll maker could even add impurities to the clay, to recreate flecking which, traditionally, has helped to confirm the authenticity of many antique dolls. Let the buyer beware!

Legitimate reproductions always bear some sort of identifying insignia. The doll artist may incise her name and the date of manufacture at the back of the doll's head. Reproduction dolls should truly be considered a distinct collecting category. They are intentionally geared toward the collector market, are usually sold in limited editions, and are seldom intended as playthings. Dolls created in the likeness of early ones deliberately to fool the public are assuredly not legitimate, nor are they valid collectibles. They are, quite simply, forgeries.

The collector who acquires a quality reproduction doll must also realize that its resale value, as well as its long-term investment potential, is unpredictable. The suggestion on the part of some sales promoters that reproduction dolls are "tomorrow's antiques" makes for lively advertising copy, but there is absolutely no guarantee that what this implies will necessarily prove to be. Then, too, a really good reproduction doll often sells for well over $200. In unusual cases, the price can run much higher. Many are turned out on a special-order basis only, with delivery taking anywhere from several weeks to several months from the time of inquiry.

These statements are not intended to discourage the collector from acquiring a reproduction doll. They are intended primarily as caveats, as food for thought, and to offer perspective. Any collector who has given careful thought to these matters and still inclines toward the purchase of a reproduction doll, should by all means go ahead and buy one.

Is segmentation (jointing) in a doll of substantial interest or concern to collectors?

The history of dolls reflects a history of experimentation and change. As doll manufacturers competed to outdo one another, they continually introduced new ideas, refined them, and then mass-produced dolls incorporating the changes to which the public had responded the most enthusiastically. This experimentation accounts for the huge volume of child dolls which appeared on the French market in the 1880's and afterward. If the 1870's was the decade of the lady doll, the 1880's was most decidedly the one of the child doll, or *bébé* (a term French doll makers used with reference to the child dolls they produced). What facilitated the enormous production of these dolls was the widespread acceptance of a ball-jointed, composition doll body. When placed between the joints of the doll at the shoulders, elbows, hips, and knees (and later at the wrists), these drilled-wood balls allowed for free and easy positioning of the doll's limbs.

Although ball-jointing in dolls was not a new idea in the 1880's, French manufacturers led the field in popularizing ball-jointed composition child dolls at that time. While it is difficult to date a doll precisely on the basis of the manner in which it is jointed, certain jointing characteristics are associated with certain time periods. Lifelike bent-limb baby dolls, for example, jointed only at the hips and at the shoulders, are associated with the early years of the twentieth century. Peg-jointed wooden dolls are associated with the late eighteenth century, although peg-jointing is actually much older. In fact, it may be traced as far back as the Greeks and Romans.

All-bisque dolls with no jointing whatsoever became popular during the mid-nineteenth century and continued in production well into the twentieth. Collectors sometimes refer to these dolls as "pillar" dolls, but more often as "frozen Charlottes," the name supposedly taken from a ballad about a young woman who froze to death one winter evening while sleigh-riding.

Figure 23. The ball-jointed composition bodies on many of the earlier dolls seem crude in comparison with the dolls' heads.

Experimentations involving the jointing of doll parts have continued into the twentieth century. Joseph Kallus made much ado about the separate neck piece used to join together the head and body of his late 1920's Margie doll. An interesting feature of the first-edition Barbie doll is the presence of metal tubes in the feet. These allowed the feet to be placed into the accommodating prongs of the first-edition Barbie's posing stand.

Just about every substance imaginable has been used by doll manufacturers as jointing material, including wood, various kinds of metal, and rubber. The collector who becomes acquainted with the manner in which different types of dolls are jointed is learning still another way of authenticating dolls, of dating them, and of determining their value.

Figure 24. With the possible exception of the string of pearls attached to the tray of the doll at left, all of the items these peddler dolls are carrying are original to them.

Can dolls serve as teaching devices?

The collector who is at first attracted to a doll because of its pretty face or because it seems somehow reminiscent of a beloved childhood toy, often develops a fascination for the circumstances surrounding the doll's manufacture. This may include interest in the processes used to make the doll itself, or in the society of its time.

A doll can upon occasion represent its times eloquently. Nineteenth-century peddler dolls, their trays loaded with jewels and notions; crisply uniformed military dolls, their guns, swords, and other weapons held aloft; elaborately gowned lady dolls, their trunks of clothes and toiletries by their sides, all these have stories to tell us. For anyone intrigued enough by a doll to investigate further, documenting dolls can become a way of documenting history.

Are unmarked dolls generally risky buys?

Unmarked dolls certainly can be risky buys, and the collector who lacks information should probably avoid them. Unmarked dolls can prove to be very fine buys, on the other hand, for experienced collectors who have done their homework. In evaluating the merits of particular unmarked dolls, the collector should be aware of the following facts relevant to doll production in the United States and Europe:

• Doll manufacturers sometimes used the same production moulds for many years. This is particularly true of the plainer varieties of chinas and parians—the ones that were inexpensively produced, and produced in great numbers. An "1850's" china could have been produced in the 1860's or even later. An unmarked doll should not, therefore, automatically be assigned a precise date of manufacture on the basis of its hair style or other supposedly telling detail.

• Very few dolls were commercially manufactured in the United States prior to the 1850's. An unmarked American doll claimed to be of an earlier period than this, should almost without exception be handmade. Any unmarked doll from before 1850 that is wearing original clothing should be wearing hand-sewn clothing.

• Many doll heads were manufactured in Germany, during the nineteenth and twentieth century, for use on commercially made dolls from other countries. An unmarked doll head is not necessarily French simply because the doll that goes with it has a French look.

• Most nineteenth-century china dolls were unmarked, and large numbers of china heads were sold loose, the remainder of the doll to be completed at home. Although the unmarked china heads were manufactured primarily in Germany, the unmarked china doll may have been completed elsewhere.

• The repeated argument that 1890 represents a safe time-dividing line between marked and unmarked dolls is open to question. While an 1890's United States tariff act did stipulate that imported goods must bear a mark indicating the country of origin, at the beginning this act did not apply as systematically or as consistently to dolls.

With knowledge of such facts as these, a collector is in a position to evaluate the merits of unmarked dolls and to determine both their authenticity and their collector desirability.

Do values of dolls change erratically?

Values of dolls change for generally predictable reasons. Most frequently, value at any given time is based upon collector interest in relation to doll availability. Although rag dolls were widely available in the 1920's and early 1930's, they sold for more at that time than did bisque dolls. Bisque-headed dolls were not the darlings of early collectors simply because they seemed too recent, too similar to what the collector may have owned and played with as a child. Early rag dolls, on the other hand, had a nostalgic appeal. The reverse is now true. While rag dolls are still coveted by collectors, they are no longer as generally well regarded as bisques, a change of attitude which is clearly reflected in current pricing.

Prices for exceptional examples of any doll defy the above logic. China dolls and the so-called "parians," with their unglazed and untinted porcelain, are considerably less prized today than bisques, unless there is something unusual and distinctive about them. Unusual chinas and parians are ones with swivel necks, with glass eyes instead of painted eyes, brown eyes instead of the more prevalent blue, or with intricate hair styling and decorative detailing instead of the familiar Countess Dagmar-type styling, with its predictable modelling detail.

Still other factors can influence doll values. Wax dolls have remained in the low-price range for years, partly because collectors assume them to be far more perishable than they actually are. Fear concerning authenticity can also affect pricing. French lady dolls leveled off in price for many years, after the market was flooded with well-made "F.G." reproductions. Lady dolls are rising in price once again, this former fear now largely allayed.

The collector who examines the shifting patterns in doll values closely will observe that prices on virtually all antique and collectible dolls have risen steadily over the years. Unless some unforeseen misfortune in the economy interrupts this pattern, doll prices are certain to continue rising in the months and years ahead.

Is it true that wax dolls make poor investments because they are so fragile?

It is this very belief that has kept prices of wax dolls low for many years. Although wax dolls are fragile, they are less susceptible to heat and cold than many collectors assume. Therefore, it is still possible to acquire fine examples at moderate prices.

Figure 25. This little poured-wax doll has survived the years virtually unblemished.

In the so-called "poured" variety, molten wax is poured directly into open moulds and allowed to solidify. After the wax has hardened, glass eyes may be inserted into cutout eye openings and secured from within. Hair is inserted, either in bunches through slit-shaped head openings, or individually, by the strand. This latter method of insertion proved much more time-consuming and, therefore, much more costly. Each hair was secured in place through the use of a hot needle.

The best wax dolls were made in England by the firms Pierotti and Montanari. The finest examples have a truly startling realism, often despite high coloring of the wax, a characteristic of the Pierotti dolls in particular. Wax dolls are seldom found with identifiable markings.

Do "X-tra" interests usually evolve from an initial interest in dolls?

Few doll collectors resist the temptation to branch out into one or more of the collecting territories which the ownership of dolls can inspire. Side interests often begin with doll accessories, such as miniature vanity sets, pieces of jewelry, or paper lithographed trunks, many of which have tray insets and lid compartments.

The collector may subsequently find a niche in any of several hobbies having to do with children, or with childhood. Nineteenth-century samplers have an appeal for many doll collectors, especially samplers that children themselves prepared, and that represent their first crude attempts at stitchery. Other collectors acquire silver feeding spoons or teething rings, many of which bear the child's date of birth, as well as intricate body motifs. Hobby horses, sulphide marbles, toy tops, bisque piano babies, and color-illustrated children's books form the basis of many sideline collections.

Early handmade valentines hold appeal, as do some of the later postcards—most particularly Kewpie postcards signed by Rose O'Neill and the Campbell Kids postcards signed by

Figure 26. Britannia tea sets sold for under a dollar at the turn of the century. This example even came with its own miniature sugar tongs.

Grace Wiederseim Drayton. Campbell Kids also appear on feeding dishes produced by the Buffalo Pottery Company. Many collectors display the dishes beside their dolls, either those of the 1910's era or the much later versions in vinyl from the Ideal Toy Company.

Paper dolls and early manufacturers' or distributors' catalogues illustrating dolls are additional collector prizes. Even so deceptively humble a document as a shipping bill for a doll can prove of interest. In my own collection, for example, is a fascinating find. It is the shipping order from 1889, for a French doll, purchased for eight-year-old Grace Carpenter. Her father, Francis Carpenter, was one of the foremost manufacturers of cast-iron toys during their heyday, the 1880's. (See page 61.)

The subject of doll extras is one which collectors of twentieth-century celebrity dolls in particular are quite familiar with. I have run across Shirley Temple doll collectors who are as interested in the Shirley songbooks, scrapbooks, and movie-theatre lobby posters as they are in the dolls themselves. Those who collect the Jane Withers doll, the Fanny Brice, the Sonje Henie, the Judy Garland, or the Deanna Durbin, avidly collect memorabilia surrounding the personal lives and professional careers of these famous stars.

It might interest doll collectors to know that the collectors of antique cast-iron toy banks will, upon occasion, pay as much for a Victorian color advertising card depicting one of these banks as they would pay for the bank itself.

The doll collector who feels the urge to branch out, might wish to read Katharine McClinton's *Antiques of American Childhood*, a well-written, richly illustrated book that deals in detail with subjects beyond the scope of this book.

Are young people becoming more actively involved in doll collecting than they were in times past?

Traditionally, dolls were saved from childhood largely out of sentiment. Not until the second and third decades of the twentieth century were dolls conscientiously acquired, displayed, and occasionally even catalogued for their historical and aesthetic appeal.

Although adults formalized the doll-collecting hobby—creating the first doll clubs, establishing the first doll shows, federations, and even prize-oriented competitions—young people have, within the past few years, emerged as enthusiastic collectors. Increased interest on the part of the young may be attributed to adult encouragement or adult sponsorship, but it is certainly also attributable to the widespread collector-credence presently accorded to plastic and vinyl dolls produced within the last three decades. Many such dolls are not only more accessible to and more easily afforded by young collectors than are dolls of an earlier vintage, but such dolls are also more likely to resemble the dolls young collectors played with during their childhood.

That young people—some in their early teens—are becoming established in the doll-collecting field is apparent. Increasing numbers attend doll shows, and they are taken seriously. Young collectors are mentioned in articles, in doll newsletters and magazines. An advertisement in *The New York Times* magazine section of October 19, 1980 predicted that in the future it may seem commonplace to find children attending auctions, exchanging catalogue notes with their parents, and making whispered suggestions relevant to the bidding.

Figure 27. *Troll dolls such as these were very popular in the 1960's and are still available at flea-market prices. Their whimsical appearance calls to mind the Kewpie dolls of an earlier era.*

Can zylonite dolls be considered the first of the plastics?

Many substances used in the manufacture of dolls have enjoyed a long reign of supremacy before passing into relative oblivion. It is noteworthy that some of the most popular doll types were advertised during their production heyday with exaggerated claims concerning their durability. French bisque *bébés* were promoted as *bébés incassables*, falsely suggesting that they were unbreakable. Dolls with composition heads made of a combination of glue, glycerine, zinc oxide, and wax, and having jointed, stuffed bodies, were first manufactured in the 1890's by The American Doll & Toy Company. The heads incorporated Solomon Hoffman's 1892 patent for "Can't Break 'Em" dolls, a misleading title, given their susceptibility to chipping and crazing. Nevertheless, over one million "Can't Break 'Em's" were in circulation in the United States by 1912, paving the way for American dominance in doll production during the years that followed the First World War.

The zylonite dolls produced by Butler Bros. in 1906 can be called the first of the plastics, although they enjoyed only a brief commercial success. The last of them appeared in 1913. The plastic on these early Butler Bros. editions was hollow, enabling the dolls to float.

Plastic-doll production did not really make headway until 1939, when Ideal Toy Corp., manufacturer of the famous composition Shirley Temple doll, introduced an all-plastic doll amid a whirl of fanfare and publicity. An article concerning this revolutionary "new" type of doll appeared in *The New York Times*.

Advertising for the early plastic dolls of the late 1930's and early 1940's again stressed their durability as a prime selling point. Time has proved otherwise; cracking, peeling, and crazing are almost as much a problem on some early plastics as they are on the compositions. Nevertheless, plastic and vinyl are currently the prime substances used in doll manufacture.

Figure 28. A grouping of modern dolls. Doll manufacturers are constantly experimenting with new modelling materials. What will follow the plastics and vinyls is anybody's guess.

3

Tools of the Trade

It is often easy to overlook the obvious. Regarding dolls, the obvious involves easily forgotten items collectors should take along when shopping for dolls. The truly canny and experienced collector prepares for a doll expedition in much the same manner that a game hunter prepares for a day of flushing out his quarry.

Just a little extra time and effort spent in planning can make a doll safari especially rewarding. The suggestions in this chapter are easy to follow, and the advice is strictly the common-sense variety. Any collector with the foresight to take along the items listed in this chapter need never return home accompanied by acquisitions of dubious value.

"Never buy a doll that you may one day have to apologize for." This advice, given to me many years ago by one of the most knowledgeable collectors of antique dolls in the United States, has served me well in more instances than I can possibly remember. In fact, I would put it first on any list of rules for doll collectors.

As recently as a year ago, I was on the verge of leaving a deposit on an unusual open-closed mouth kid-bodied German doll. She had lit-

tle teeth, delicately etched within the open-closed mouth arrangement. The expression on her face was wistful and slightly pouty. The price was inviting. It was a tempting buy.

But then, holding the doll up to the light and illuminating the head from within with a small pencil-type flashlight, I noted the surface bisque was scarred and pitted. The pitting was not bad, in comparison with that on some dolls. Still, it was bad enough to reduce the collector appeal of the doll considerably, rendering the acquisition inadvisable, after all. I might eventually have made a profit selling the doll, since values have been climbing steadily over the years. Nevertheless, there was no way that I could honestly say that the doll was in pristine condition.

Selling a doll with pit marks on the face means beginning with an apology, and that places the seller in an uncomfortably defensive position. This point is taken from the perspective of a doll dealer, because every collector is a prospective dealer—even beginning collectors. Every collector reaches a point where a particular doll no longer appeals, or when, in order to acquire a coveted doll just a bit beyond the collector's means, it becomes necessary to part with one or more lesser examples.

The doll with the pit marks on the face would not be one a collector could trade or resell easily.

When speaking of items essential to have when doll hunting, a small, pencil-type flashlight is crucial. I am surprised at how many otherwise knowledgeable collectors are unaware that a sharply focused light will not only set off surface flaws but will also, when properly inserted into the head cavity, illuminate the bisque (all fine doll bisque is translucent, incidentally). Interior illumination will reveal any repairs or restorations. Do not confuse the opaque facial areas (places where plaster has been internally applied to set eyes or to secure other mechanisms) with restoration work. Check for opaque spots on the chin, cheeks, around and behind the ears, at the back of the head, and near the crown. On solid-dome doll heads, insert the light through the opening at the base of the head or neck.

Keep in mind here that no reputable doll dealer would knowingly operate dishonorably. Dealers who value their reputations will be most careful to advise customers of any faults a particular doll may have. If it is a dealer in general antiques, however—someone who upon occasion happens to have dolls in stock—the dealer may himself be totally unaware that he is carrying damaged or restored merchandise. Also, many general dealers will be loath to permit removal of the head and shoulder plate on dolls that do not have open crowns. If this happens, get it in writing that if the doll is not exactly as described, you may return it for a refund after you have had a chance to examine it.

Nowadays even damaged desirable dolls are selling for high prices. Of course, a doll's value is greater when the damage is off the face and hidden from view. Longtime collectors may bristle at the fact that some repaired dolls now cost what dolls in flawless condition cost just a few years ago. Ten years ago, a perfect Bru could have sold for $2,000. Currently, a repaired Bru of the same type could sell for considerably more than that. Prices have escalated, and collectors must learn to adjust to this and not feel displeased with their acquisitions simply because the doll market has changed.

A damaged doll should never sell for the going price of a similar doll in pristine condition, though. Whenever the purchase of a damaged doll is being contemplated, the prospective buyer should think about and answer the following questions: Is this a doll that I plan to keep? Am I buying this doll for immediate or eventual resale? Am I willing to go through the bother (and the expense) of restoration? Do I have access to a competent doll restorer? Should I buy this doll now—especially if it is in the hard-to-find category and is attractively priced—with the intention of trading up at some future time if an example in superior condition to this one happens my way?

The collector may not have the answer to every one of these questions at the point of purchase, but should nevertheless be aware of the questions themselves, and should not buy either in haste or in a state of confusion.

How big is the doll? It seems inconceivable, but there are doll dealers in shops and shows who do not indicate the exact size of the doll on the price tag. Occasionally, dolls have been measured improperly. The owner of a doll from a private home may not even know the exact size of the doll. When the matter of an inch one way or another can make a difference of perhaps $100 or more on the current market, it is best to take no chances. Ask to measure the doll. No reputable seller will be affronted by such a request.

Figure 29. Even when dressed as simply as she is here, the Bru doll transmits an elegance that is unmistakable.

47

For measuring dolls, a wooden ruler is out of the question because of its inflexibility. Also out is anything hard or potentially abrasive that could snag the doll's clothing or mar the surface of the doll. A cloth measuring tape is therefore the best alternative.

When measuring a doll, stretch it out on a table, being certain to adjust the head if it is a socket-headed doll and to smooth down the legs at the knees if the knees are jointed. Measure up the back of the doll from the base of the feet to the crown opening, or to the very top of the head if the head is the solid-dome type. This will give you the most realistic dimensions. Shoes, socks, and elaborate hats should not be included in the measurement.

These measuring instructions refer to toddlers and adult dolls. Bent-limb baby dolls may be measured this way, but sellers of these dolls often give the head circumference as well

as the body length. In order to get an accurate rendering when measuring the head, place the tape directly above the doll's ears and move it over the brow and around the back at the widest point or bulge. Since both head size and body length can affect a doll's pricing, always bring along a measuring tape when doll shopping.

"I just got it out of an attic," the dealer tells you in a hushed voice. *"See, it's still all grimy from the old trunk it was stored in."*

While such a story may bring smiles of disbelief to the knowledgeable or slightly jaded collector, the fact is that dolls do upon occasion emerge from private homes or estates. When they do, especially if they have been left untouched for a number of years, time may have done its work in terms of dirt, worn stringing and jointing. Additionally, the eyes may have become detached from their moor-

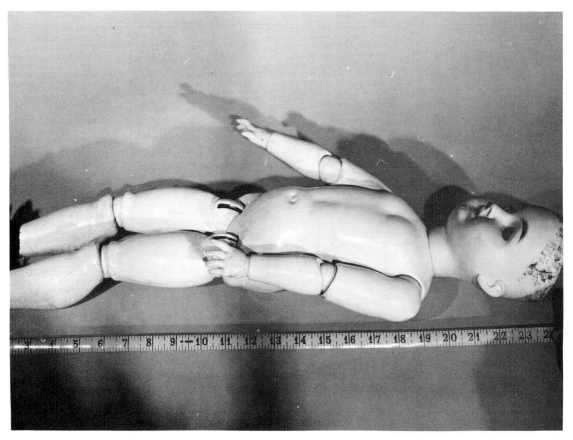

Figure 30. Measuring a doll.

ings and may be rattling around loosely within the head cavity. The clothing may be stained or badly worn.

Still, such a doll may prove to be a very good buy indeed. Dirt and grime, however, may camouflage flaws. If the seller really did just acquire the doll and has not bothered to present it to you at its party best, a bit of fast work with a damp cloth (the kind that comes in waterproof envelopes) will quickly release all but the most stubborn grime, and will reveal the true condition and quality of the doll.

Be cautious when doing any cleaning on a doll, however. A few years back I sold a wasp-waisted, open-mouth Jumeau to a novice collector who telephoned me in a state of panic a few days after the sale. She accused me of having misrepresented the doll because when she washed the back of the doll's head, the Jumeau lettering washed off as well. The label in question was a stamped, red-marked *tête Jumeau*. Suffice it to say here that any such stamped lettering would prove highly vulnerable to a liquid or a powder abrasive.

"Do you want to carry it, or shall I just place it in a shopping bag?" I had just started collecting dolls. How I carried the doll home seemed far less important to me than did the fact that I had just made a fine buy on a Grace Putnam Bye-lo baby. The seller, a relatively new dealer also, shrugged at my apparent nonchalance, put a bit of tissue around the doll's head, and placed it, head-down, within a paper shopping bag. I shall never, ever forget the sickening sound of splintering bisque which I heard when I returned home and lost my grip on the bag. The damage was so severe as to be irreparable.

I have, however, saved that doll as a perpetual reminder to myself never to leave the house on a doll jaunt without bringing with me the following additional items: a large, sturdy canvas bag with canvas handles, packaging tape, white tissue paper, and disposable diapers. These diapers are particularly good for wrapping (separately of course) the head, limbs, and body of the doll. They cushion the doll while it is in transit, protecting it against breakage, and also preventing the limbs from rubbing against the body and creating scuff marks. If such a procedure seems too costly, or too precautionary, then at the very least see to it that the head of the doll is well padded and is placed head-up—never head-down—within the packaging.

If the doll is to travel any distance and is one of the sleep-eyed variety, it is always best to remove the wig and to stuff the head cavity with tissue paper, thereby reducing sharply the chances of the eyes falling into the head. This can happen far more easily than a beginner might suppose, for the plaster matrix holding the eyes in place, on older dolls in particular, can prove extremely weak and brittle. Once you have the doll safely home, be especially careful when removing the tissue from the head. Never wrap dolls in newspaper. Newsprint can easily rub off onto a doll and prove difficult to remove, both from the doll and the doll's clothes.

Since that heartbreak over the Bye-lo, I have never lost a single doll to breakage, even when I have sent dolls long distances through the mails. As the result of a freak experience at a doll show, I have, however, devised still one additional precaution. When I examine a doll for possible purchase, I always check to see that the doll has been correctly strung. By "stringing" in a doll, I am referring to the slim, elastic-like bands within the doll, which keep the limbs and head properly attached to the body. Many older dolls, and even some newer ones, need restringing from time to time. The original elastic loosens in time or simply disintegrates from age. However, the restringing must never be so tight as to cause undue internal tension. All the buyer really has to do is cradle the doll protectively, pull gently at the limbs, and gently again at the head. A socket head should move easily, but not too freely. On the other hand, if the head is totally immobile, and if the limbs are so stiff as to be virtually immobile also, the doll has been too tightly strung and should not be purchased until the seller has made the necessary adjustments.

At this particular doll show, the dealer her-

Figure 31. 1920's baby out for a stroll.

self was pulling at the back of a beautiful, closed-mouth Jumeau doll head in order to allow me thorough inspection of the doll's markings. Suddenly, with no warning whatsoever, the head of the doll popped right off the body, arched gracefully through the air, and landed in pieces on the showroom floor. The strings had simply snapped from the slight additional pressure that had just been applied. This doll had been restrung only the day be-fore the show and, as the dealer realized too late and much to her chagrin, far too tightly. As a further commentary on what has been happening to doll values recently, the same doll, beautifully restored (and so marked on the price tag), appeared in the booth of the same dealer one year later—at the exact price that it had been marked when I first saw it in still-pristine condition. It sold!

Figure 32. Twenty-four-inch (60-cm) closed-mouth, fully marked, late-nineteenth-century brown-eyed Jumeau.

Figure 33. Twenty-nine-inch (72.5-cm) German bisque with brown sleep eyes. She has a ball-jointed body, a blonde human-hair wig, and is marked "JDK 214."

OTHER USEFUL ITEMS

The list of things to carry along could, of course, extend indefinitely. As in all other matters related to doll collecting, however, common sense should dictate the limits. Take along a high-grade magnifying glass to enlarge doll facial details and to check for minute flecks or chips around the eye and ear areas and between the upper lip and the base of the nose. A magnifying glass will also come in handy when you try to decipher the sometimes-difficult-to-distinguish incisings on the back of the doll's head, incisings which often identify the doll manufacturer, mould size, and style number. Extremely faint incisings may indicate that the doll was the product of an old and worn mould. If this is the case, facial detailing may be affected and the collector should re-examine the doll from this standpoint. Note in particular the sharpness and clarity of the ear modelling when making such an assessment. Once again, pricing on the doll is a factor here.

Nail-polish remover is surprisingly effective in eradicating traces of glue at or near the crown opening. The glue, used to secure the doll's wig, may mat the hair. The hair then adheres to the bisque or composition doll head and makes accurate examination of the doll difficult unless the glue is at least partially dissolved and the hair pushed aside.

A hairnet is excellent for keeping the wig neatly in place while your doll is in transit. The mohair fibres used on some early doll wigs, and widely used on the twentieth-century celebrity dolls of the 1930's and later, mat quite easily.

PROPER SHOW CONDUCT

A pencil and pad will always come in handy for taking dealers' names and telephone numbers, as well as other information which you might easily forget. A sale initiated in a dealer's booth at a show may be finalized by mu-tual agreement at a later time, most often at the dealer's home. Most dealers are receptive to doing business this way. There is a distinct advantage for both buyer and seller in negotiating in an atmosphere of complete calm, where each has the other's total and undivided attention. The dealer who objected to a customer's removing glue from a doll's crown at a show, will most probably not object to such a procedure at home. Also, dealers generally have dolls at home which they did not bring to the show. Sometimes, one of these dolls will be available for sale, and will appeal to the collector more than the original doll.

Never feel embarrassed, whether you are at a show, in a shop, or even at a dealer's home, about taking out a price guide and checking it for information pertinent to the doll you wish to purchase. Price guides are by no means sacrosanct, but those which have been carefully prepared by reliable and knowledgeable authorities on dolls will prove invaluable even if all that is provided, in a given instance, is a rough estimate of the going price of a doll. Most dealers refer to price guides as a matter of course when determining the amounts they hope to secure for their dolls. Since price guides are generally well-stocked with photographs, it is always satisfying to compare the photo with the actual doll. Always check the copyright date of the guides, and keep in mind that guides give prices from some time prior to publication. The prices on many dolls, therefore, may be higher than those in the price guide.

A camera, provided that you make your reasons for picture taking clear to the dealer, is a real plus whenever you are out sleuthing for dolls. Some dealers may be understandably sensitive about your snapping flashbulbs within the booths of a doll show. Also, dealers will catch on quickly if you are simply comparison shopping or are out to accumulate pictures for your files. If you explain that you have a real interest in a particular doll and that you would like a clear picture of the doll while you are contemplating the purchase, most dealers will understand and will accommodate

MASTER CHECK LIST FOR DOLL SHOPPERS

1. Pencil-type flashlight

2. Cloth measuring tape

3. Moist towelettes

4. Magnifying glass

5. Sturdy canvas bag(s)

6. Disposable diapers

7. *White* tissue wrapping paper and masking tape

8. Hairnets

9. Nail-polish remover

10. Camera (optional)

11. Doll price guide

12. Pad and pencils

you. But again, lurching from booth to booth at a doll show, snapping pictures indiscriminately, smacks of an intrusiveness that from all standpoints is totally out of order.

Negotiations with a dealer should always be conducted with diplomacy and tact. I have witnessed occasions where thoughtless collectors have planted themselves in the middle of a dealer's booth during the most active hours of a show, monopolizing a dealer's attention with trivia and showing little or no regard for the dealer's business. Most doll dealers truly love dolls and are ardent collectors, but there is a time and a place for everything. A doll show is definitely not the place to tell a dealer a story about what happened to a doll you inherited from your Aunt Jenny.

Finally, if you do request permission to examine a doll and the dealer is agreeable, it should take you no more than a few minutes to follow the suggestions in this chapter.

TABOOS

Although the theme of this chapter is what to take with you when out doll shopping, there are a couple of things to leave behind. Do leave behind your very young children. While it is a joy to see young people expressing an interest in dolls, nothing is more exasperating to dealers at a show, as well as to shoppers, than a small child running around out of control, fingering dolls, colliding into tables, or complaining loudly about being tired and wanting to go home. Any collector who can afford an antique or collectible doll can afford a sitter for an infant or toddler.

Also leave behind your best friend, whose wisdom in dolls you may wish to honor while deliberating between two dolls that you have seen at a show. As often as not, the friend is no expert at all, and will simply confuse you with irrelevant questions and suggestions, thereby dampening your enthusiasm and causing you to return home, either troubled about what you bought or empty-handed. If you have done your homework—as you should before making even your very first purchase—you need no one but yourself and the dealer to negotiate a sale.

Figure 34. Flirty-eyed German with two-tone open mouth and human-hair replacement wig.

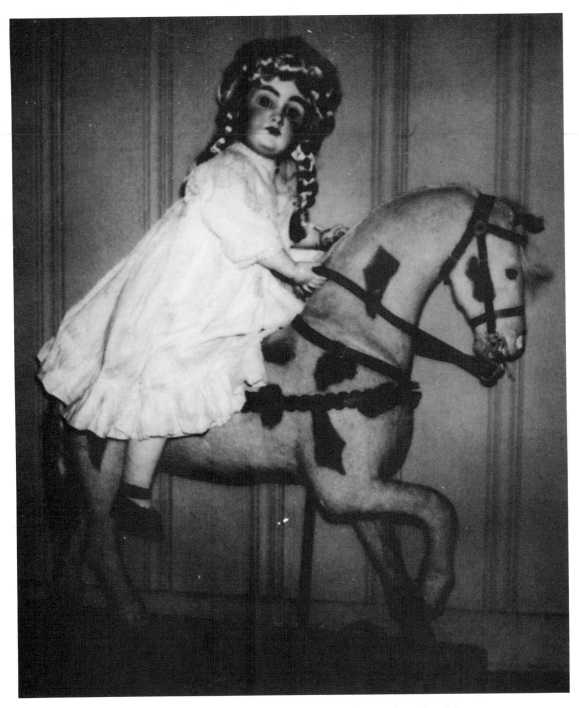

Figure 35. A lively and interesting way to display a favorite doll.

~ 4 ~

Establishing and Expanding a Collection

All doll collectors can recall the excitement, mingled with confusion and self-doubt, which typified their early years of collecting. Some dolls acquired by a beginner prove to have been worthy of acquisition, but more often than not, they prove to have been bad buys. Not only does the beginner lack knowledge about dolls in general, but also experience sufficient to make informed decisions of a comparative nature. A collector may, for example, have the impression that all china dolls look alike, unaware that many distinctive and unusual chinas were produced over the years. A collector may also have the impression that all dolls produced by the same manufacturing company and bearing the same markings look alike, unaware that variations often occurred through long-term use of the same moulds, or through differences in facial detailing hand-applied at the time of manufacture.

With limited knowledge and limited experience handling dolls, the beginner is more likely to be swayed by surface allure than by any other factor; a pretty doll face or pretty doll clothing may be the most compelling motives behind a purchase. While a doll's appearance is always of great importance, it is by no means the only factor—or even the most im-portant factor—to influence the seasoned collector who is contemplating still another doll acquisition.

Other important concerns invariably include the condition of the doll, its comparative scarcity, and the reputation of the manufacturer, as well as the originality of all component parts. The experienced collector also considers how much a potential doll addition will fit into an existing collection, how much room there is for additional dolls, the size of the doll under consideration, and even the type of differences between the doll in question and those the collector already owns. An experienced collector may also buy a doll at a modest price, either for the purpose of trading with a dealer or fellow collector, or to sell for outright profit.

In short, there are many matters to consider while acquiring dolls. As a collector gains in experience, the decisions become harder, and more challenging. Eventually, the collector may branch off into a specialized area of collecting. Seldom does specialization render decision-making simpler. In fact, the more highly specialized the collection becomes, the more fine-haired are the decisions the collector confronts.

SOURCES OF DOLLS

The advanced collector has generally worked out over the years a reliable network of buying sources. The beginner is seldom at such an advantage, and is frequently burdened not only by ignorance about dolls, but also by a lack of information about how best to acquire them. Establishing a collection is simply not possible until the collector has his sources.

"*Where do I go in order to acquire most easily the dolls I wish to collect?*" As might be anticipated, there is no easy or foolproof answer. If the collector lives in a large community, or even in a community of modest size, there may well be a "doll lady" of local renown. Such a contact will serve as a good starting point, if not for the actual purchase of more than a doll or so, then for the information which such people are generally gracious enough to share with an eager but sincere beginner. By "doll lady," I am referring to a woman who has herself been a collector for many years, who knows dolls thoroughly and loves them, and who participates actively in doll clubs and doll shows.

Never expect such a person—or any dealer in dolls for that matter—to reveal buying sources. What you can expect, however, is advice regarding the dolls she herself may have for sale, or advice regarding the dolls which may be available through her from among her many collector and dealer friends in the area. I recall one such doll lady who advised me, quite shrewdly as it turned out, to check the "for sale" section of small-town newspapers whenever I was out of state and in a position to do so. She claimed that some of her best

Figure 36. Some collectibles on display at the New York Doll Hospital.

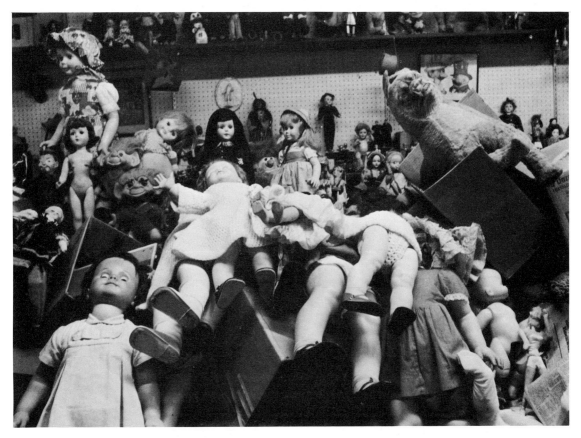

Figure 37. Dolls at the New York Doll Hospital.

buys came from this procedure, especially during winter months, because during the off-peak seasons, and especially during precarious economic times, many homeowners run sales that may include the more recent collectible dolls.

Aside from doll shows, which are always a good source, many towns have at least one doll hospital or repair shop. Collectors often find that making periodic visits is both educational and rewarding. Shops that deal exclusively in dolls are generally found in large towns or cities only. For a beginner, a visit to a doll shop, a doll museum, or even to a doll exhibit can be well worth the time it takes to get there. Even when dolls on display are not for sale, the more dolls a collector can look at, touch, examine (most likely to be permissible in a shop, and seldom, of course, permissible at a museum or exhibit) the better the

collection ultimately will be. No matter how many books a collector may read or pictures a collector may look at, nothing can equal the experience of seeing and holding an actual doll.

Doll lists published by private dealers, as well as those advertised in trade journals, are also excellent buying sources. There are, in addition, dealers who could be called wholesalers. These are people who buy and sell dolls on a grand scale and who shop for their merchandise both nationally and abroad. It is not uncommon for them to buy dolls in lots of hundreds, and to buy entire collections of dolls all at one time. Such dealers are often amenable to doing business directly with the private collector, even though this means but a single sale. The purchase may be the first of many, and the dealer is well aware of this.

Doll auctions are still another source, but I

Figure 38. Inspection time at Auctions By Theriault.

would advise the beginner to attend several before attempting to acquire in this manner. Many of the major auction houses now conduct periodic doll sales, a commentary on the degree to which doll collecting has become a big business. Even if the competitive, rapid-fire proceedings which take place at the actual auction make the inexperienced collector feel weak in the knees, attending auctions can prove instructive.

Doll auctions are customarily preceded by a preview, a time when prospective buyers examine the dolls. In addition, the literature from auction houses contains a wealth of information. Advance-of-sale catalogues include predicted prices for the dolls and accessories up for bidding. Following the auction, listings of the prices dolls actually fetched at the sale are generally available, enabling the collector to remain informed concerning buying trends on the current market. Often the auction catalogues present such detailed descriptions and photographs of dolls that they serve as miniature encyclopedias, well worth retaining as a part of the collector's permanent doll library.

Some doll auctioneers now extend their sales to include lecture sessions, doll seminars, and appraisal clinics. While there may be a modest fee for participation in these activities, the opportunity to obtain advice about dolls represents a good buy as well as a sound investment, and may more than justify the price of admission.

The inexperienced collector should take a few precautions when buying dolls. Resist temptation whenever in doubt about the merits of a particular doll. Few dolls are so uncommon that a comparable one will not turn up at a future time. Never be pressured into believing that unless you act quickly you will be giving up the chance of a lifetime. Truly exceptional dolls are their own best sales representatives. They do not require hawkers.

If you somehow become convinced that unless you have a particular doll under your arm you cannot leave the premises, at the very least ask the seller to indicate in writing, along with the date and the price of purchase, that the doll is returnable for full refund within a specified number of days if it is at variance with the condition described on the sales slip. If the seller suddenly becomes hesitant or is unwilling to make such a commitment—and sign his name to it—the new collector has all the information needed to avoid a financial tragedy.

Figure 39. Shipping receipt for a French doll. This receipt is discussed on page 41.

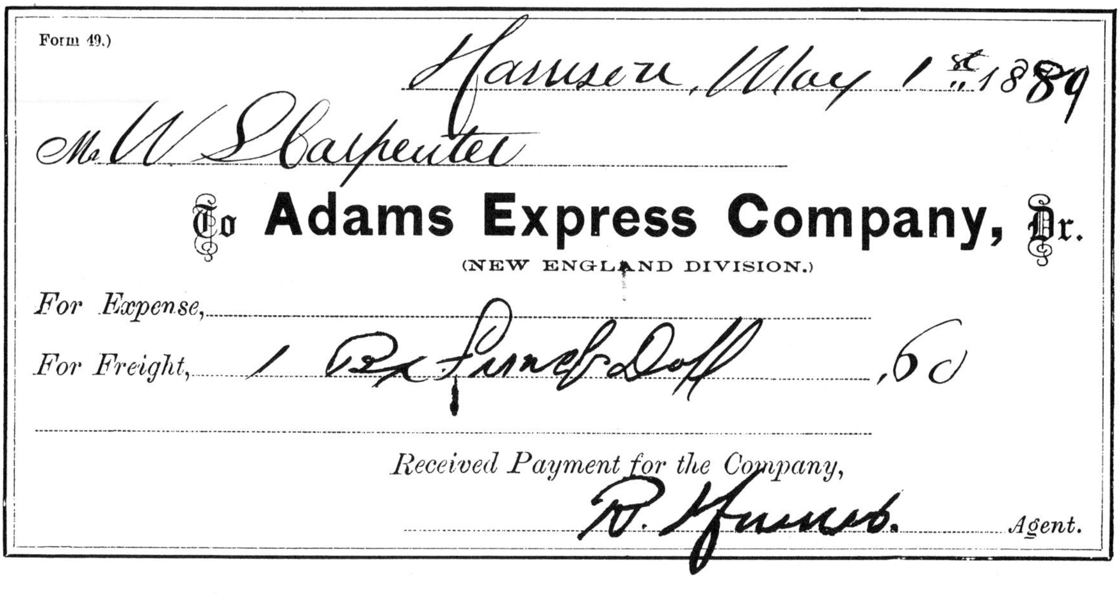

None of this precautionary information is intended to dampen a collector's enthusiasm about acquiring dolls. Still, collecting should proceed in a spirit of fun, adventure, and relaxation. There is no pleasure in finding out that a doll you brought home with you in high spirits was fundamentally unworthy of the purchase.

Richard W. Withington, Inc.

Presents At Auction

The Doll Collection of the Late
DOROTHY E. THOMPSON of Waldwick, New Jersey
Plus Selections From Other Collections

Friday, November 21 and Saturday, November 22, 1980

at the
New Hampshire Highway Hotel, Concord, New Hampshire
at 10:00 A.M. each day

Partial Listing: Kissing Bru — Jumeaus — JDK — Googlie — All Original Set of Dionne Quints — Chinas — Heubachs — K*R — Schoenhuts — Byelos — French Bisques — German Bisques — Fashion Dolls — Bald Bisques — Armand Marseilles — Wax over Compositions — All Bisques — Simon and Halbigs — Revalo — Baby Dolls — Kewpies — Dollhouse Dolls — Miniature Dolls — Greiner — Doll Heads — Kestners — Bonnet Head Dolls — RARE RUBBER K*R — Madame Alexander Little Shaver — Dollhouses — Georgene Averill — Chinese Theatre Figures — Shirley Temples and MORE!

NO ABSENTEE BIDS ACCEPTED

Inspections:	Thursday, November 20	8:00-10:00 P.M.
	Friday, November 21	8:00-10:00 A.M.
		8:00-10:00 P.M.
	Saturday, November 22	8:00-10:00 A.M.

Catalog $5.00   Price List $2.00

Sample catalogue pages from a Richard W. Withington, Inc., doll auction. The prices quoted on page 65 are the actual prices the dolls fetched at this show.

RICHARD W. WITHINGTON, INC.

Presents At Auction

The Doll Collection of the Late DOROTHY E. THOMPSON of Waldwick, New Jersey

Plus Selections From Other Collections

NO ABSENTEE BIDS ACCEPTED

TERMS OF SALE: All items MUST be inspected and returned within 10 minutes of
purchase and be of $100.00 valuation or more to qualify for re-
fund if not as described in the catalog. ALL BOX LOTS and LOTS
are AS IS. All items designated as AS IS are FINAL SALES. Due
to the sufficient time allowed for inspecting the dolls, all
bodies are as described in the catalog. If they are original to
the head or not is up to the buyer to decide.

1. 25" china shoulder head, unmarked.
    Black molded curly hair with bow and band (slight wear), painted/molded fea-
    tures, cloth body, leather arms, dressed.

2. 19½" china shoulder head, unmarked.
    Short black curly hair (wear), painted/molded features (pocked), cloth body,
    wood limbs (wear), dressed.

*3. 17" bisque character head boy marked with Heubach sunburst 76 DEP 04 7 33
    Germany.
    Painted/molded hair, blue intaglio eyes, molded open/closed mouth with molded
    teeth and tongue, (slight wear on cheeks), jointed composition body (new),
    dressed.

4. 20" (13½" circ.) bisque head baby marked K*R Simon & Halbig 116A 50.
    Sleeping blue eyes, molded open/closed mouth with two teeth and tongue, (paint
    chips under wig around crown), wig, composition bent leg body (paint wear),
    dressed.

5. Lot of two vinyl head doorstops, Old Farmer and His Wife.

*6. 21" bald china shoulder head, unmarked.
    Slot in top of head, blue glass eyes, closed mouth, (cheek wear), wig, cloth
    body, leather arms (worn), dressed.

7. 16" all wood boy marked Schoenhut.
    Carved hair, incised eyes, closed mouth, (wear on head), spring jointed all
    wood body (paint wear), dressed.

8. 13" bisque head marked 5.
    Sleeping blue eyes, closed mouth, wig, new jointed composition body, socks and
    shoes only.

9. 15½" (10" circ.) rubber head Byelo marked Grace Storey Putnam.
    Painted/molded hair and features (sticky), cloth body (soiled), rubber limbs,
    dressed.

10. 11" (8¼" circ.) bisque head baby marked Copr. by Grace S. Putnam Germany.
    Painted/molded hair, sleeping blue eyes, closed mouth, new cloth body, cellu-
    loid hands, dressed.

11. 14" wax over composition shoulder head doll. As Is.

*12. 19" bisque head marked FG in a scroll.
Brown glass eyes, closed mouth, pierced ears (nicked), wig, jointed composition body marked Jumeau Medaille D'Or Paris (paint wear, fingers chipped), dressed.

13. 13½" bisque shoulder head fashion marked 1.
Blue glass eyes, closed mouth, swivel neck, wig, kid body (soiled and patched), undressed.

14. 12" bald (3 hole) bisque head unmarked.
Brown glass eyes, closed mouth, (cheek wear, black specks on face), pierced-in ears (nicked), wig, jointed composition body, dressed.

15. 5¼" tall parian-like bisque shoulder head only, unmarked.
Blonde molded hair, center part, three curls on each side of part to ears, soft curls in back falling below braided coronet on top of head, painted/molded features, pierced-in ears, cloth body and clothes in separate bag, (body as is.).

16. 20" vinyl head doll, unmarked.
Sleeping blue eyes, inset light brown hair, swivel neck, young lady type body, dressed.

17. 22" (15" circ.) composition head baby marked E.I.H. Co. Inc.
Painted/molded hair, sleeping blue eyes, open mouth with teeth, flange neck, cloth body, composition limbs, (all composition crazed), dressed. As Is.

18. 24" bisque shoulder head marked No. 3500 AM 8 DEP.
Blue glass eyes, open mouth with teeth, no wig, (shoulder broken and glued), kid body (soiled), bisque lower arms, undressed.

19. 19½" (14" circ.) composition head baby marked Ideal Doll Made in USA.
Painted/molded hair, flirty sleeping brown eyes (splattered), open mouth with teeth, cloth body (soiled), composition limbs, (all composition worn and crazed), undressed.

20. 19" wax over composition shoulder head, unmarked.
Brown glass eyes, closed mouth, wig, (wear on head and shoulders), cloth body, composition arms, dressed.

21. 10½" bisque shoulder head, unmarked.
Short blonde curly hair, painted/molded features, cloth body (as is), bisque limbs (finger chipped, legs broken off), Original Clothes.

22. 8" bisque head marked Globe Baby DEP Germany 3/0 H.
Brown glass eyes, open mouth with teeth, wig, crude composition body (wear), undressed.

23. 6" all bisque marked Germany 2.
Blue glass eyes, closed mouth, no wig, rigid neck, jointed at hips and shoulders, painted/molded socks and shoes, (slight chips on tops of legs), undressed.

24. 8" bisque head marked S&C Simon & Halbig Germany 18.
Sleeping brown eyes, open mouth with teeth, no wig, composition straight limb body (paint wear, left foot off), dressed.

25. 5" bisque head marked 139.
Blue glass eyes, closed mouth, no wig, composition straight limb body (wear), Original Clothes.

26. 4½" all bisque marked 4.
Blue glass eyes, closed mouth, wig, swivel neck, jointed at hips and shoulder painted/molded socks and shoes, (needs restringing), Original Clothes.

Richard W. Withington, Inc., Auctioneer & Appraiser

SPECIALIZING IN ANTIQUES AND FINE FURNISHINGS

PAGE 1

HILLSBORO, NEW HAMPSHIRE 03244, TEL. 603-464-3232

	PRICE LIST			DOLL AUCTION			NOVEMBER 21 & 22, 1980	
1. $ 120	46. $ 25	91. $ 250	136. $ 70	181. $ 325	226. $ 90	271. $ 1025
2. 75	47. 25	92. 70	137. 310	182. 275	227. 3150	272. 410
3. 450	48. 25	93. 140	138. 25	183. 85	228. 250	273. 80
4. 1600	49. 40	94. 40	139.] 50	184. 70	229. 1100	274. 160
5.	50. 30	95.] 65	140.]	185. 25	230. 1150	275. 2700
6. 2050	51. 45	96.]	141. 530	186. 600	231. 875	276. 3200
7. 400	52. 25	97. 45	142. 790	187. 310	232. 375	277. 2100
8. 625	53. 25	98. 45	143. 270	188. 150	233. 3100	278. 25
9. 130	54. 30	99. 80	144. 110	189. 70	234. 3100	279. 75
10. 210	55. 200	100. 4500	145. 375	190. 575	235. 100	280. 45
11. 65	56. 70	101. 900	146. 325	191. 110	236. 520	281. 35
12. 1475	57. 55	102. 2150	147. 650	192. 400	237. 50	282. 60
13. 775	58. 60	103. 45	148. 950	193. 275	238. 260	283. 65
14. 525	59. 300	104. 380	149. 950	194. 1100	239. 40	284. 500
15. 525	60. 170	105. 220	150. 1200	195. 2550	240. 290	285. 425
16. 25	61. 70	106. 1200	151. 1050	196. 25	241. 200	286. 160
17. 35	62. 80	107. 110	152. 1150	197. 600	242. 100	287.] 100
18. 120	63. 55	108. 110	153. 90	198. 325	243. 130	288.]
19. 40	64. 190	109. 170	154. 40	199. 750	244. 130	289. 600
20. 110	65. 140	110. 650	155. 65	200. 3700	245. 140	290. 160
21. 45	66. 180	111. 600	156. 55	201. 2300	246. 160	291. 260
22. 120	67. 925	112. 170	157. 170	202. 1700	247. 120	292. 45
23. 55	68. 375	113. 80	158. 55	203. 450	248. 110	293. 50
24. 50	69. 60	114. 160	159. 50	204. 210	249. 420	294. 55
25. 100	70. 150	115. 250	160.] 70	205. 400	250. 60	295. 25
26. 130	71. 220	116. 2050	161.]	206] 130	251. 105	296. 280
27. 90	72. 180	117. 500	162. 75	207]	252. 120	297. 280
28. 110	73. 200	118. 550	163. 50	208. 250	253. 240	298. 200
29. 25	74. 70	119. 110	164. 100	209. 240	254. 160	299. 2600
30. 230	75. 290	120. 2200	165. 50	210. 25	255. 25	300. 1600
31. 260	76. 450	121. 160	166. 60	211. 30	256. 45	301. 1400
32. 1150	77. 550	122. 310	167. 65	212. 1350	257. 55	302. 200
33. 1850	78. 280	123. 190	168. 50	213. 35	258. 40	303. 3100
34. 225	79. 200	124. 550	169. 350	214. 45	259. 90	304.] 25
35. 360	80. 150	125. 2650	170. 350	215. 50	260. 75	305.]_
36. 350	81. 310	126. 325	171. 65	216. 50	261. 400	306.] 60
37. 150	82. 110	127. 130	172. 45	217. 60	262. 110	307.]_
38. 230	83. 2850	128. 330	173. 45	218. 100	263. 525	308.] 40
39. 130	84. 475	129. 110	174. 40	219. 85	264. 70	309.]_
40. 370	85. 45	130. 130	175. 50	220. 35	265. 80	310.] 25
41. 375	86. 800	131. 130	176. 40	221. 25	266. 25	311.]_
42. 160	87. 225	132. 325	177. 175	222. 120	267. 160	312.] 25
43. 110	88. 160	133. 160	178. 525	223. 75	268. 2300	313.]_
44. 35	89. 80	134. 250	179. 250	224. 90	269. 1400	314.] 55
45. 80	90. 40	135. 155	180. 250	225. 55	270. 200	315.]

MAIL ORDERS

Doll lists and mail-order catalogues are good sources for dolls. The reader may be wondering whether acquiring via the mails is not a risky procedure. Some of my very best purchases have come about as a result of answering ads. I can remember no moment more exciting than when, telephone in hand and a doll periodical open before me, I got first claim on a 1930's composition celebrity doll, fully tagged and in its original clothing. Return privileges are customarily extended to all mail-order purchasers, providing that the doll under consideration is returned within a limited time period (usually three days to a week) and is in the same condition it was when it was sent out.

To avoid disappointment when sending away for dolls:

1. *Never send a check for a doll without first ascertaining that the seller still has it.* Remember that thousands of collector-subscribers are likely to have spotted the same ad, and the doll may well be gone by the time your check arrives. Therefore, telephone the dealer. In this way, you will not only determine the doll's availability, but you will also be able to question the dealer closely about things that may be important to you, but which the dealer may not have included in the ad.

For example, an ad might read: *18″ (45.7 cm) Shirley, fully marked, all original clothes and wig, fine condition: $600.*

Fine condition, you may discover, means that there is slight surface crazing to the composition on the side-cheek areas, that the eyes have faded and have been oiled to restore their original color intensity, and that portions of the body have been repainted. Whether or not you still wish to order the doll, given these drawbacks, is then up to you. There are collectors who will refuse a doll if the body has been repainted, but have no objection to some surface crazing.

2. *When sending written inquiries to a dealer about a doll, keep your letters short and to the point.* You may inquire about the feasibility of budget terms for purchasing, providing the dealer has mentioned this possibility in his ad, but do not haggle over the price or suggest terms of your own choosing for payment. Most dealers work on a very narrow margin of profit these days, and advertising is expensive.

3. *Do not expect dealers to contact you every time they acquire the sort of doll you are collecting.* While most dealers are happy to keep a list of what you want on file, your own requests—especially if they pertain to the highly collectible dolls—coincide with those of many others.

4. *If you must return a doll, mail it back immediately.* Many dealers have several back-up customers waiting for the same doll you ordered. The doll should be double-boxed and well insulated against breakage. Dealers will also request that the doll be returned via first-class mail, and insured. Some dealers "absorb" mailing costs by not charging extra when mailing a doll out to you. If you are returning a doll, however, the costs involved are your responsibility.

5. *If you are ordering from a new dealer, or from an unknown dealer, you have every right to ask for bank references before mailing a check for a doll.*

Collectors sometimes ask whether dealers get special consideration on the dolls they buy. This is generally the case under special circumstances only. For example, a dealer may make an exception for a colleague who has sent business his way from time to time or has offered leads on dolls. However, the standard dealer discount of ten percent is actually less than that which a dealer might accord to a customer of long standing. The advantage dealers do have over private collectors comes

Figure 40. Although wedding cake figures like these by Simon & Halbig do not count as dolls to most experts, many doll collectors nevertheless enjoy owning them.

at doll shows, for during the set-up period which precedes the official sale time, dealers have access to all dolls first. Buying and selling and trading among dealers at the shows is always vigorous.

PRICING

To what extent are the published price guides truly indicative of current doll values? How does a collector know how much to pay for a particular doll? With the exception of where to buy dolls, the question which troubles most beginning collectors concerns the correct amount to pay for dolls once they have been located. There really never is a "true" price or a "fixed" price for any doll or for a quality antique in any of the various categories.

Someone once said that the real price of an antique is the price a particular buyer is willing to pay for it at the moment of purchase. There is some truth to such an observation. Even if ten price guides were to suggest that an 18-inch (45.7-cm), fully marked and tagged Shirley Temple should sell in the neighborhood of $600, this is still simply an estimate. It is a price based on observations made at antique shows and auctions, in general antique shops as well as in doll shops, from doll dealer lists and ads in doll periodicals.

As the authors of responsible price guides readily admit, the collector must be knowledgeable enough about the variables that can influence pricing to make an informed decision at the point of purchase. The collector must know, for example, that the published prices in the guides are generally for dolls in good-to-excellent condition, with all original parts, and of very good-to-superior quality. Damaged dolls, dolls with replacement parts, repaired dolls, and dolls of poor quality (one eyebrow painted higher than the other, for example, or disconcerting facial specking), should sell for considerably less than the published prices, under most circumstances.

A doll in its original factory box, on the other hand, one that is in a perfect state of preservation as a result of never having been handled or played with, should sell for far more than the listed price. Collectors of modern dolls are just as aware of this as are collectors of antique and collectible dolls. While most Barbie dolls can still be obtained for in the neighborhood of $20 to $25, the original 1959 edition is currently valued at over $500, *if* it is in mint condition and in its original Mattel Toys box. The 1959 Barbie, out of the original box, but still in pristine condition, would fetch under $200 at the present time.

Never to be underestimated either, in the price a collector is willing to pay, is a doll's own particular appeal. A collector may have examined ten #211 Kestner character babies within a year's time and turned them all down. Then one day at a doll show, one priced conceivably a bit higher than those already examined, one with an undefinable appeal to its facial expression, tugs at the collector's heartstrings and says, "I'm the one."

Dolls do vary from example to example—even dolls from the same factory, and bearing the same mould numbers. Never feel ill at ease or in the least foolish for paying a bit more for a doll than you may originally have intended. The doll may well be worth every extra dollar you found yourself willing to pay for it.

On the subject of paying for dolls, it is important for every collector to set limits. Some collectors have cheerfully dined on spaghetti for a month in order to accumulate funds for a doll they had reserved for purchase. Perhaps this is admirable. It certainly is not admirable, however, if securing a doll means skimping on essentials or entering a state of financial distress.

Most dealers are amenable to reserving a doll, provided the collector leaves a deposit. The deposit is typically one-quarter to one-third the cost of the doll. Anywhere from three months to a year is generally allowed to pay the balance—this depending upon the price of the doll, the dealer's willingness to hold items, and the collector's credit.

I know of no dealers at the present time

Figure 41. The hollowed-out body of this candy-box doll by Heubach pulls apart to reveal the storage space for sweets.

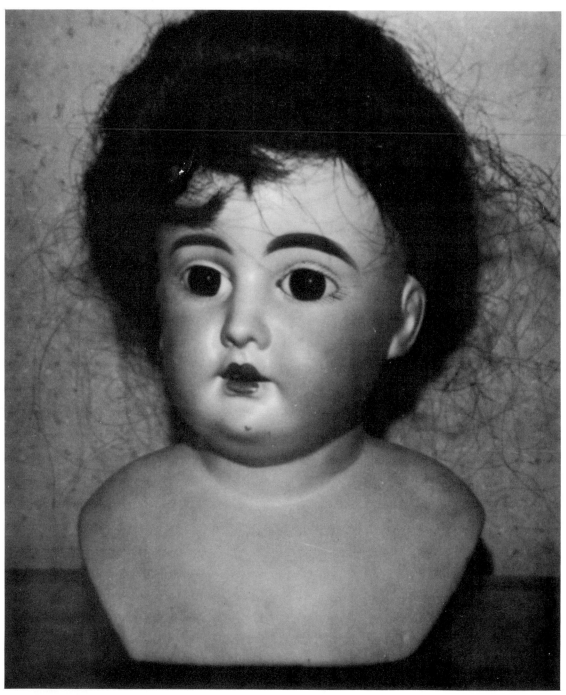

Figure 42. Dolls like this German turned-shoulder-head are still available in the moderate-price range.

who charge interest on time-payment doll purchases. The collector's advantage is obvious, particularly if the time allotment extends beyond three months. Even if the value of the doll goes up appreciably during the layaway period, the collector is required to pay no more than the initially agreed upon figure. Installment buying can therefore prove to be a shrewd way of buying, even for the collector of considerable means who wishes to exercise financial prudence and at the same time acquire several choice but expensive dolls. Some dealers accordingly limit both the number of dolls and the time allowed for paying for them. Many dealers will also stipulate that dolls acquired this way are not returnable.

GETTING STARTED

Even after locating doll sources and securing the funds for doll purchases, the beginning collector may have difficulty getting started. An initial experience with dolls can pave the way. If a family heirloom doll has sparked the collector's interest, seeking variations in type from the doll inherited is a good way to begin. The collector who has been attracted to dolls as a result of an interest in fashion or fashion trends may seek out dolls whose clothing is representative of their period of manufacture. If the attraction to dolls is based on the collector's love of children, acquiring baby dolls, dolls with smiling faces, or toddlers may be the answer.

However, even with an initial idea of where to start, few beginners have more than a hazy idea where their collecting interest is leading them, or how to proceed along the way in order to avoid risk and disappointment. While all beginning collectors are destined to make mistakes, some the inevitable result of inexperience and many essential to the learning process, there are precautions *all* collectors should take to avoid expensive errors:

• Avoid badly damaged dolls, especially if the damage affects the facial areas.

• Avoid buying dolls with even minor damage, with the intention of having such dolls repaired, *until you have investigated the going rates* doll restorers in your area charge. Do not consider such purchases unless the cost to you will not be out of proportion to the initial cost of the damaged dolls.

• Avoid buying a doll whose wig or shoes seem impossible to remove. The seller may be trying to discourage you from locating areas on the doll that have been damaged or restored. One unhappy collector of choice French dolls paid top dollar for a beautiful, marked Bru. When she finally succeeded in removing the shoes, she discovered crude clay stumps, rather than feet! (She returned the doll and fortunately got her money back.)

• Avoid dolls whose heads seem too big or too small for their bodies. You may be looking at a doll mongrelization. The head of one doll may have been incorrectly attached to the body of another.

• Avoid buying doll parts on the assumption that you can locate the rest of the doll at some future time. This may turn out to be far more difficult than you had supposed. In more cases than you might imagine, your wait for the missing parts will be interminable.

• Avoid pleading ignorance. You are simply inviting people to take advantage of you.

• Avoid pleading poverty or asking for special consideration on doll prices. A doll is strictly a luxury purchase. There are more buyers for good dolls than there are good dolls available to buy. Leave your crying towel at home—or word about you will get around and you will find most doors closed to you.

• Avoid buying too many dolls too quickly out of an initial enthusiasm. Your tastes may change in time and, if you are just a beginner, you may not as yet know how dedicated a doll collector you are.

• Avoid letting your enthusiasm or pride in your purchases loosen your tongue concerning the contents of your doll collection, its value, or its whereabouts. Aside from accidentally breaking a doll, nothing is more sickening than coming home and finding them gone. There has been enough publicity about doll prices to make dolls a tempting target for burglars. This does not mean that you should never mention your dolls in public. It simply means that you should be discreet as to when and where you discuss your dolls, and with whom.

DOLL PARTS

A few of the preceding precautions are subject to qualification, and no one of them, except the last, should be taken as absolute. A damaged doll may indeed warrant acquisition if the doll is in the hard-to-find category and the damage is off the face. Keep in mind that broken fingers on composition-bodied dolls, and broken toes (as well as most other forms of minor body damage) will not diminish the value of a doll appreciably, except in the eyes of uninformed sellers.

Figure 43. A grouping of dolls gains special interest when all the dolls are of a similar type (in this case, babies).

Figure 44. The appeal of these dolls lies in the way they "play off" against one another—in height, in head and body treatment, and in facial expression.

While collectors should be alert to the possibility of a doll mongrelization, some "errors" in doll assemblage may have occurred many years ago, during the time that a doll was in the possession of its original owner. Collectors familiar with early toy catalogues, as well as with the catalogues of such distributors as Marshall Field, Montgomery Ward, and Sears Roebuck, can attest to the fact that doll parts could be ordered retail from any one of several suppliers. The 1907 edition of the L.H. Mace & Company toy catalogue indicates that they had in stock the following doll replacement parts: china heads, bisque shoulder-heads, bisque socket-heads, rubber-doll heads, metal and celluloid heads, muslin bodies with bisque forearms, jointed kid bodies riveted at the hips, dolls' arms—the upper part of kid and the forearm of bisque—and dolls' wigs. Every one of these items came in a broad range of sizes, but it is most probable that in at least some instances a mother would order or receive an incorrect size. It may have mattered very little at the time, either to the child or to the mother who mended the doll, whether or not an ordered part fit the doll precisely. The important thing was to fix the doll so that the child could play with her again.

These factors are worth remembering, particularly to lay to rest the theory that doll dealers everywhere are indiscriminately throwing parts together, whether the parts are appropriate or not, simply to finish off an otherwise incomplete doll which they may have acquired. No reputable dealer would even contemplate such a thing.

A dealer may indeed feel that a doll part is worth acquiring under certain circumstances. Fine and unusual doll heads are always of interest, particularly china and parian heads. Collectors of these doll types frequently display just the heads, even when they are in possession of the complete doll. This may be partly to economize on space, but it may also be because the primary interest, in the better examples of these dolls, is in the elaborate detailing and ornamentation of the heads, and sometimes of the shoulder plates.

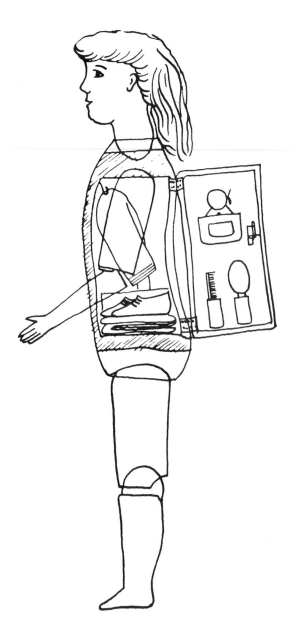

Figure 45. Drawing of Mechtold and Chillingworth's 1894 mechanical doll with wardrobe in body. (From Gwen White, "European and American Dolls and Their Marks and Patents". B. T. Batsford, London, 1966.)

An unusually fine doll head in any of the established collecting categories would similarly be worthy of acquisition, providing that it can be acquired at an advantageous price. I know of one young collector who obtained an impressively large and beautiful closed-mouth Bru doll head for well under $100, a paltry sum when one considers that the complete doll would currently fetch in the neighborhood of $8,000. This collector displays her Bru proudly in a clear plastic case, and many collectors who own matching Bru bodies wish they could buy the head from her.

The more recent the doll, the less likely the collector would profit immediately from acquiring separate parts or from repairing major damage. While there is increasing buyer action on French and German doll heads with hairline cracks, there has not yet been much action on damaged plastics and vinyls. This situation is destined to change as the demand for these later dolls continues to rise and the supply gradually diminishes. Many modern and collectible dolls are already in the hard-to-find category, and they have increased in value at a faster rate than authorities on pricing anticipated even a single year ago. This is particularly true of some of the celebrity dolls of the 1930's and 1940's.

DISPLAYING DOLLS

Techniques for displaying dolls effectively interest all serious collectors. If the collector is affluent, it may be possible to set aside an entire room in a home as the doll room. This is generally a room that becomes so filled with dolls and doll accessories that eventually there may be little space to move around. The advantage of such a room is that dolls can be displayed unprotected with minimal risk of breakage. The disadvantage is that the collection is isolated, and is enjoyed in the one location only.

I prefer positioning dolls throughout a home in such a manner that they seem less like

a formal collection than like an integral, life-like part of the household decor. The lifelike look is achieved by placing dolls in antique strollers or carriages, by seating them on child-sized sleds, rocking horses, swings, or high chairs, or by positioning them in groups around miniature tables set with doll-sized tea sets or dinner services.

Dolls may also be displayed holding hands, or holding baskets of dried flowers, toy musical instruments, Teddy bears, or even smaller dolls. A large doll, seated on a chair or rocker in the entranceway of a home not only provides a pleasing touch, but also quietly announces the presence in the home of a doll collection. Secure straps or rope, carefully con-

Figure 46. Eighteenth century "penny" wooden tuck combs.

Figure 47. A teddy-bear convention. Collectors often enjoy pairing teddies and dolls.

cealed beneath a doll's clothing and attached to whatever prop has been selected to pose the doll, provides for a doll's safety. Another idea, particularly suitable for displaying small chinas or all-bisques, is to enclose them in shadow boxes and then to arrange these on a wall. The effect is particularly interesting with small dolls with original wardrobes and accessories. These may be carefully mounted to the background of the box, surrounding the doll.

Never create such a crowded effect when displaying dolls that they become indistinguishable from their backdrops or from one another. Dolls jumbled together in display cases, bumping elbows and knees, sometimes bring to mind disgruntled commuters on a rush-hour train. There is no justification for such crowding. If necessary, rotate your dolls periodically, rather than displaying all of them at once.

PROTECTING DOLLS

There are several other matters to consider when selecting display areas for dolls. Some antique fabrics, particularly the silks, are vulnerable to strong light. Dolls dressed in these materials should not be placed in direct sunlight. They should also be kept away from drafts, as well as from extreme or rapid shifts of temperature. Since they prove irresistible to babies and many household pets, dolls should be placed beyond their reach, in conventional display cabinets or under glass domes, if necessary.

The novice collector may not know it, but there has long been an affinity between antique doll bodies and clothing and the kinds of tiny insects and moths that can easily enter a home undetected. Placing small containers filled with moth crystals at discreet intervals within doll display units will discourage insect activity. Similarly, small containers filled with water in identical fashion will provide your dolls with life-preserving moisture in rooms that are too dry or are simply overheated.

To compensate for the strong scent moth crystals impart, and to enhance their moth-repelling qualities, you may wish to place herb or spice mixtures around your collection. There are many opinions about which herbs and spices most effectively discourage pests. The French have traditionally used Artemesia (southernwood) to protect clothes; a Mexican method of repelling moths is to sprinkle ground pepper on woollens before placing them in an airtight trunk. (Because of the tightness of the wood, cedar chests have long been used to protect clothes.) Heather is also considered an effective herb to guard against clothing damage. Herbs are used separately or in combination, generally in small cloth bags which are placed on or near the items to be protected.

There appears not to be any scientific research comparing the effectiveness of moth crystals and strong-scented herbs or spices for discouraging insects, however, and certain spices—such as paprika—attract bugs. Therefore, be sure to consult a reliable herb manual before deciding which to use in your collection.

Other ways to discourage insects from invading a collection are to air out dolls and doll clothes in bright sunlight, to shake or vacuum clothes gently to remove eggs, larvae, and dead moths.

While I have suggested that dolls achieve a greater effect in animated settings, placing dolls behind glass may be the answer if the collector is a specialist and wishes to draw attention to the many variations there are within a single doll category. Set up neatly behind glass doors, a collection of French F.G. lady dolls or American Barbie dolls gains more impact when dolls are placed side by side than when they are separated from one another and scattered randomly about the house.

The side-by-side effect will highlight subtle differences in hair coloring and style, facial expression, size of dolls, and their manner of dress.

Unless the collector elects to display her dolls seated in strollers and chairs or securely strapped to hobby horses or other attractive mountings, the safest thing is to utilize the commercial posing stands, which are currently available in a wide range of sizes. The armatures of these stands, as well as the circular bases, can usually be concealed within the doll's clothing. In instances where concealment is impractical, the collector can soften the effect by carefully covering the metal parts with fabric. Fabric coverings also protect the finish of the doll against rust and abrasion where the stand comes into direct contact with the doll's body.

Figure 48. This doll has been preserved in her original condition.

Figure 49. Re-dressing a doll may enhance its eye appeal, but this does not necessarily enhance its value. In contrast to the elegantly re-dressed lady dolls in this figure, the doll in Figure 50 may seem dingy, even dilapidated. Still, someone at a doll convention thought enough of her all-original condition to award her a blue ribbon—straggly wig, roughened cheeks, worn dress, and all!

Figure 50.

Figure 51. German child with painted-on shoes and socks.

No matter how the dolls in a particular collection are displayed, proper cataloguing should begin with the first doll acquired. A small file—the sort used for recipes—will do. Data for each doll should be placed on 3″ × 5″ index cards. How the information is recorded is again a matter of collector preference, but a file card will typically include the following information:

- Factory name and/or mould numbers. A tissue-paper "rubbing" of an incised marking is easy to make, and can be taped to the back of the card.
- Type of doll—bisque, composition, vinyl, or other—noting any differences between construction of doll head and body.

- Size of the doll.
- Eye type—set eyes or sleep eyes—as well as eye color and shape.
- Wig type and color.
- Manner of jointing.
- Mention of damaged or restored areas, as well as of replacement parts.
- Manner of dress, including brief description of fabrics and whether they are original or later replacements.
- Date and source of acquisition.
- Amount paid for the doll at the time of acquisition.

A small, color photo of each doll should, if possible, be pasted on the front or back of each index card.

K*R (Kammer and Reinhardt)   Doll's
                                                              photo
Mould #117

Bisque head made by Simon & Halbig

Sleep brown glass eyes, closed mouth, ball-jointed composition body

Height: 17 inches (43.2 cm)

Original brown, human-hair wig

Hairline at back of head, professionally restored

Original socks, shoes, and underclothes; collector-replacement blue cotton dress and straw hat

Acquired: J. Jones, dealer, June, 1979

Price: $2,000

Such records will prove valuable both to the present collector and to the person who eventually buys or inherits the doll collection. Careful record keeping is also useful for insurance purposes. Prudent collectors keep a duplicate file in a bank safe-deposit box.

Prudent collectors also keep an alphabetized, cross-indexed file of all matters pertaining to their doll-collecting needs. This file should be so arranged that, at the flick of a finger, the collector can verify any one of the following details:

1. The names, addresses, and telephone numbers of collector and dealer acquaintances who actively buy, sell, and trade dolls.

2. The names and locations of dealers who stock fabrics, shoes, stockings, wigs, and earrings appropriate to specific doll types and doll production periods.

3. The names, locations, and calendar dates of doll shows, exhibits, and auctions which the collector habitually attends.

4. The titles of books and articles in the collector's doll reference library, with pertinent annotations concerning facts of interest.

If such record keeping seems to the beginning collector too extensive, remember that experienced collectors find that detailed files on all aspects of doll collecting lend interest and scope to a collection, save time, and—not to be minimized—keep the collector happily occupied between doll purchases. How much more informed present-day collectors would be if all collectors in years past had kept detailed records of the acquisition and maintenance of their dolls.

Looking ahead, it is entirely plausible that at some time in the future collectors may acquire their dolls with the help of a computer. Mr. Kim McKim of Kimport Dolls, in Independence, Missouri, claims that his long-established and highly respected firm is considering the possibilities of computerizing a nationwide dealer-collector service. For a small fee, collectors could have their specific doll wants placed on computer tape. Dealers would also have their inventories placed on tape. With the aid of the computer, buyers and sellers could then be matched quickly and accurately.

Some collectors become uneasy at the notion of such a system, but it does have many advantages. Computerized buying would be a boon to collectors who live in romote areas, who are elderly, or whose livelihoods preclude regular visits to shops, shows, and auctions. As Mr. McKim explained, such a system would in no way affect the many courtesies for which reliable doll firms such as his are world-famous. Kimport, as many readers know, is the publisher of the highly informative and educational bi-monthly magazine, *Doll Talk*.

In addition to retaining original doll clothing, everything original to the doll should be retained. This would include an original wig, for example, if the collector has replaced it. It would also include the original doll box, if there was one.

It is best to tag original items and pin them inconspicuously to the undergarments of the doll or to a concealed portion of the doll stand. Once due note of this has been made on the doll record card, the chances of the original items becoming lost or separated from the doll they belong to are virtually nil. More advanced collectors, incidentally, are likely to retain straggly looking wigs and tattered clothing, if they are originals, rather·than to replace them.

Beginners who discard original items, or who rush to repair shops to have timeworn dolls completely repainted, are generally sorry later. Not only have they irrevocably altered the original doll; they have under most circumstances also diminished its value.

Collectors who are either just beginning or who are actively expanding their collections often ask whether there are still good buys on the current doll market. Although it is true that dolls in general have tripled in price within the past ten years, only a few have

Figure 52. The conventional manner of displaying dolls. Space permitting, they would look better under less crowded conditions.

accelerated at a faster rate than this. These few are primarily the closed-mouth French *bébés*, and uncommon doll examples in other categories. "Uncommon" means a doll which seldom emerges on the market, such as a factory-boxed all-bisque doll with several original outfits still pinned to the inside lid. French lady dolls, complete with original trunk, accessories, and a lavish ensemble of outfits, corsets, and hats, also command high prices.

There are, however, some dolls that have not kept pace with inflationary trends and would make good buys today for the generalized collector. These include chinas and parians. Such dolls were popular thirty or

PRACTICAL
HOUSEKEEPING

WITH DOLLS

THE Cranford Doll Houses offer the newest, most unique and educational ideas ever brought out for the pleasure and training of children, and a long felt want is amply met in these practical and artistic creations. The houses are built after designs of colonial and modern houses, decorated and furnished with the same care and study for artistic effect as is used in planning and furnishing the houses in which we live. While much progress has been made in children's toys in the past few years in the way of new and more practical things and a broadening in educational features, still there has been little or no advancement made in the doll house itself. It is the same cold, hideous, inartistic thing it has always been—a poor imitation, lacking the prime essentials. Every advancement in children's toys seems to have favored the careless, rollicking boy, while the future mother of a busy household has had to rest contented with improvised doll houses and furniture. playing mostly with things representing houses and furniture which would almost as easily represent anything else.

It has long been the study and serious consideration of the head of the novel idea of the Cranford Doll Houses how this sad lack in girls' play-things could be met and advanced to the position it should hold, and how "playing dolls" could be made most instructive and educational. This idea has been so well carried out in the plan of the Cranford Doll Houses that the young mistress has been brought in the most fascinating manner face to face with practical housekeeping with dolls—the foundation stone of the domestic building completed in after years.

On other pages are pictures of some of the houses we are pleased to offer the public and on which we solicit its endorsement and patronage. They are all well made of the best selected and well seasoned lumber, with shingled roofs, latticed windows opening out, or colonial windows with green shutters, miniature stairways and doors which open and shut. They are painted and artistically papered and furnished, being complete miniatures of the houses from which they are copied.

They are supplied with the necessary dolls completely dressed, and with the proper furniture for each room. All of the houses are worthy the serious consideration of every mother, and the Cranford Doll House Company will be pleased to correspond with anyone interested in these houses and give any particulars or further information that may be desired. From time to time new designs and models will be built embracing a price range that will be most gratifying to those interested in these houses.

Cranford Doll House Co.
207 MICHIGAN AVE., ✀ CHICAGO

CRAIGIE HOUSE—INTERIOR

Miniature reproduction of Long-fellow's Cambridge home. Color buff and white with green tile roof and green swinging shutters. Contains 12 rooms. Stairway from first to second floor. Front and back both removable, giving the child ready access to all rooms. All fitted, decorated and furnished complete, including draperies, cur-tains carpets, furniture, tester beds chintz couches, and a complete family of dolls, including servants. The most unique and remarkable doll house ever produced.

Size 2 feet 7 inches high, 2 feet 6 inches deep, 4 feet 1 inch wide.

Complete, ready for use, $125.00

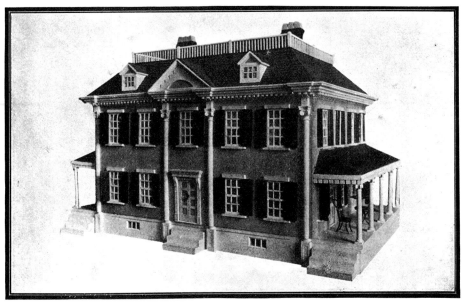

Truly fine dolls and toys were often expensive, even many years ago, as this early twentieth-century advertisement indicates.

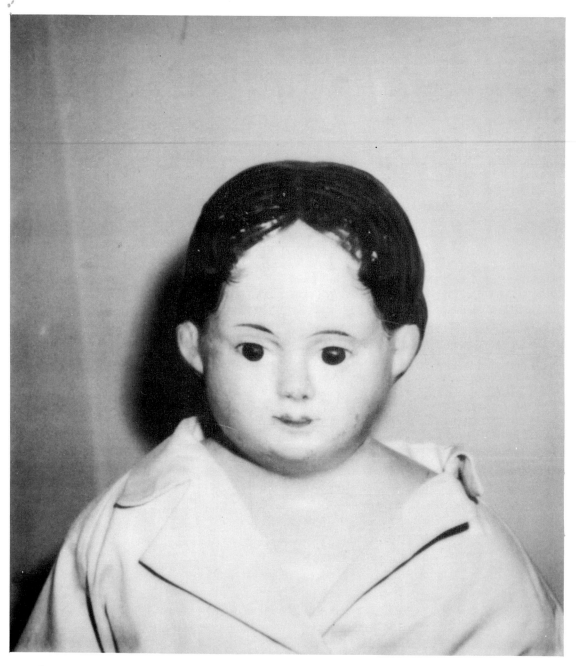

Figure 53. A fine example of a doll in the still-moderate price ranges. This one is a Greiner, and has its original, 1858 (patented) paper label.

forty years ago, but recently seem to have lost their mass appeal. While exceptionally unusual chinas and parians currently do fetch prices of $1,000 and over, many fine and interesting examples are still available for well under $500. It seems inevitable that collectors will rediscover the beauty and the charm of the chinas and parians, so these dolls are "sleepers" on today's market. Other doll types worthy of being collected and still quite moderately priced are the waxes, the milliner's models, the papier mâchés (such as those manufactured by Ludwig Greiner of Philadelphia), and the kid-bodied, turned shoulderhead Germans. Curiously, there is a tendency to consider all of these German shoulderheads as adult dolls, and to dress them accordingly. In actuality, the ones with plump necks and cheeks, as well as unusually short bisque forearms, were intended to represent infants and should be dressed in christening gowns.

Collectors who persist in expressing dismay over current doll prices should try to remember that many dolls sold for relatively high prices at their time of manufacture. Jumeaux dolls dressed only in chemises sold for upwards of $20 shortly after the turn of the century. With elaborate, commercially made or couturier outfits and accessories, the price could become $100. This was at a time when the average wage earner made only ten or fifteen dollars a week. An early 1900's ad for a doll house manufactured by the Cranford Doll House Company of Chicago, pictures a completely furnished and finely detailed model of the poet Longfellow's Cambridge home. The house was for sale at $125. Translated into current economic terms, the figure becomes approximately $1,200. Truly fine toys were never cheap.

Several years ago a well-known dealer suggested giving up her doll business because the Jumeau had reached a going rate of $175. "It's all over," she mourned. "Who would pay $175 for a French doll?" Time has proven otherwise. The knowledgeable collector should not be discouraged by today's prices. Collectors in the year 2000 will undoubtedly wish they could buy their dolls at the 1980's rates. Collectors just beginning, or advanced collectors seeking fresh collecting territory, should give serious consideration to the acquisition of plastics and vinyls, many of which have also appreciated in value, along with the earlier compositions and bisques. Current celebrity dolls, limited-edition dolls, and advertising dolls, especially if they were produced in small quantities (such as the Sunmaid-Raisin doll), will also make fine investments.

One of the joys of collecting is the knowledge that anywhere, at any time, even during the current doll boom, a good buy on a choice doll is still within the realm of possibility. The collector must simply know dolls, know which questions to ask, and which pitfalls to avoid.

Figure 54. Note the variety in height, and in facial expression, within this grouping of black dolls. All four are bisque-headed, with composition bodies.

∿ 5 ⌒

Specializing

Sooner or later almost every collector develops a keen interest in a particular doll type or category or manufacturer and begins to specialize. This does not necessarily mean that the collector ceases to acquire dolls outside this specialty. It simply means that the challenge of seeking out special dolls becomes one that urges on the collector. The possibilities for specializing in dolls are almost infinite. No one chapter in a doll book could possibly detail them all. What this chapter does, instead, is to comment on some interesting possibilities for today's collector to consider, most particularly for the collector who may never have given more than passing thought to the subject of specialization.

The more advanced the collector, the more definitive the tastes of the collector-turned specialist. One noted collector developed such a fascination for the early American rubber dolls produced in the nineteenth century by such companies as Goodyear and the Newark India Rubber Company that she parted with some of her choicest French bisques in order to obtain the rarest and the most perfectly preserved examples. Since most of the early rubber dolls have held up poorly—the rubber

cracking or solidifying with the passage of time and the paint chipping to such a degree as virtually to obliterate facial detailing (see page E, #1 & 2)—such dolls would presumably seem crude, ugly, and totally undesirable to the average collector.

I mention this to emphasize a point about specializing that might not occur to new collectors. Specialization allows the collector to give expression to tastes and interests which may initially seem unrelated to doll collecting. Fashion, design, art, history, music, and dance, as well as the cultures of various countries and diverse ethnic groups by implication or association, are relevant to dolls and to the circumstances surrounding doll production. It is interesting and significant that within the past few years museums across the country have begun to include antique dolls for display purposes. It again demonstrates that dolls have cultural as well as aesthetic merit—merit which has until quite recently been widely ignored.

The pictorial survey in this chapter suggests the diversity of choices possible. Of course, actual choices must be made by the individual collector. How the collector proceeds to establish a specialty depends as much upon ingenuity as it does upon any other factor, including doll cost and availability. Certainly no authority on dolls has the right to dictate boundaries for specialized collecting— any more than to do so regarding generalized collecting. The only ground rule would be that the dolls within a selected area of specialization be united in some identifiable, thematic way.

Thus, in addition to those categories selected for inclusion on the following pages, the collector might specialize in so specific a category as brown-eyed chinas or in so general a category as baby dolls. Other possibilities would be military dolls of diverse historical periods, bride-and-groom dolls, "bonnet" bisques, or all-bisques. A collector might concentrate on the dolls of a particular manufacturer, such as the prolific Heubach, or of a particular era, such as the 1930's. There is virtually no limit to the categories a collector might devise.

Again, the pictures and discussion in this chapter should be considered a starting point, intended to interest and stimulate the imagination rather than to define boundary lines.

ORIENTAL AND BLACK DOLLS

The popularity of the Oriental doll in the late nineteenth and early twentieth century coincided with the emergence of interest in the customs and culture of the Far East. Vigorous trading with the East brought to the Western world the sumptuous silks, the carved rosewood and teak, as well as the ivory and

Figure 55.

Figure 56.

jade for which the Orient had long been noted. Oriental design left its signature on the late Victorian home in terms of richly carved pedestal tables, throne-back chairs, folding screens, and hand-stitched and embroidered silk tapestries. By 1900 there was scarcely an upper-middle-class home that did not boast an ivory carving on the whatnot or a jade figurine among the cut-glass compotes in the china cabinet.

Nowhere is the relationship between the doll world and the world of fashion and design more clearly apparent than in the grouping depicted in Figure 55. The dolls themselves, many dressed in original and authentic Oriental costumes, are all-bisques. They range in size from just under 3 inches (7.6 cm) to just over 7 inches (17.8 cm). Of particular merit are the undressed, pixie-faced "ping

Figure 57.

pong" (second from right) and the 6½-inch (16.5-cm) unmarked JDK Oriental with his smiling, character-type expression, slightly open mouth with teeth, and multicolored silk outfit (Page C, #3). Of equal merit, however, is the elaborately carved Oriental furniture grouping which complements this display. A close-up of the throne-back chair (with 5-inch [12.7-cm] doll with original wig and painted-on slippers), indicates the precision with which miniature furniture was at one time fashioned (Figure 56). Such furniture, with its delightful animal motifs, would surely be of as much interest to the art historian as to the doll collector (Figure 57).

Many of the leading French and German doll firms produced the fine Oriental dolls prized by today's collectors. A distinctive few of these dolls, notably those manufactured by Kestner, Schoenhau & Hoffmeister, and Simon & Halbig, were from newly designed moulds. They duplicated the facial contours of the Oriental with impressive authenticity. Other dolls of the period were, at best, simply yellow-tinged remakes of dolls already in production. They offered little beyond flesh tone or hairstyling or dress to suggest the Eastern influence. While such dolls may be striking in appearance and may be of considerable value —an Oriental Bru, for example, with eyebrows painted diagonally across stock mould lines (see page 35 for a reproduction of just such a doll)—Oriental-doll collectors prize in particular those dolls which reveal the racial characteristics as a structural part of the basic mould design. A case in point would be the extremely slant-eyed unmarked doll in Figure 58. The modelling is well executed, and the doll has her original outfit, consisting of a multicolored tunic over pants, trimmed with braid. The black mohair wig is also original, and very long. She sports a coolie hat.

The 16-inch (40.6-cm) Oriental (Page F, #1) is also of particular interest. Marked SH 1199 Dep, she has her original black mohair wig, open mouth with four teeth, pierced ears, and brown sleep eyes. The bisque is colored a deep brown, suggesting biracial origins. The

Figure 58.

slanted eyes are accentuated by the dramatic arch to the brows. She is dressed in her original factory outfit of yellow and red cotton, with yellow ribbons at the waist and on the hair. She has a jointed, composition body.

The 14-inch (35.6-cm) Lenci Oriental (Figure 59) is in felt, as is characteristic of this twentieth-century maker. The doll has her original Lenci cloth and paper labels, original black hair, and the brown painted eyes with pupil highlights. The middle and fourth finger of each hand are sewn together, again in characteristic Lenci fashion. The most decidedly Oriental feature of the doll, aside from the costume, consists of the high, butterfly-wing eyebrows.

While less Oriental in look or feel than other dolls depicted in this section, the 13-inch (33-cm) Belton (Figure 60) is unquestionably choice. She has three holes in her pate and stiff wrists—both Belton characteris-

Figure 59.

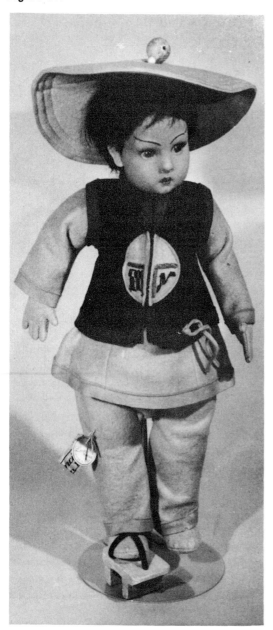

Figure 60.

Figure 61.

tics. Marked simply "220," her replacement clothes are of little consequence. What elevates this ball-jointed composition doll in both interest and value is the combination of Belton and Oriental influences. The eyes have a slight tilt at the corners; the complexion is yellow-tinged.

A favorite always among Oriental-doll collectors, the #243 JDK (Kestner) baby in Figure 61 is richly dressed in what appears to be a ceremonial outfit. Thirteen-and-one-half inches (34.3 cm) in height, he has sleep eyes with painted lashes above the eyes only, an open mouth revealing two teeth, and a long hair braid hanging down the back of his neck. He originally came as one of a pair, the girl doll dressed similarly, but in contrasting colors. Assuredly this doll represents the quintessence of Oriental-doll manufacture. No other example captures quite so much character appeal as he does, without sacrificing any of the detail which suggests his Eastern origins.

The 11-inch (28-cm) Chinese noble (Figure 62), dressed in his original outfit, trimmed with silver filigree appliqué, is another example of an Oriental doll in which the features are rendered with a portrait-like accuracy. He has a composition head and hands on a wire-armature body. The headdress is moulded on, with the hair painted forward over the temples. His Chinese boots are also moulded and are painted black and white with heavy white soles. He stands on a base of wood covered with multicolored paper. The doll is unmarked.

As realistic in portraiture as the Chinese noble, is the 14-inch (35.6-cm) coal black with bisque head and jointed, composition body (Page F, #2). Marked 1368 Germany, S&H 4, she is a fine example of an early doll with decidedly Negroid features. She has the original black, curly mohair wig, an open mouth with four teeth, and moulded brows. Her dress, straw hat, and red shoes are collector replacements.

Figure 62.

95

Note the contrast in representation between this doll and Page F, #3. While the 23-inch (58.4-cm), open-mouth Jumeau is unquestionably desirable in this chocolate edition, she is in fact simply a brown version of a standard and familiar Jumeau mould.

Until the past few decades of the current century there was genuine, but by no means consistent, interest on the part of manufacturers in producing black dolls and toys that were racially distinctive, however stereotyped and negative. Some early dolls, like the Jumeau under discussion, were merely black-faced replicas of the Caucasian model, but early tin and cast-iron toys in particular went to extremes in depicting blacks negatively—as comical, featherbrained, or jazz-crazy. An 1880's mechanical bank was known as "The Jolly Nigger." A later tin toy composed of a black male doing a soft-shoe on a rooftop was called "Jazzbo Jim." Rag dolls through the years, as well as the various editions of Aunt Jemima, portrayed blacks as working-class, happy-go-lucky folk with bandanas on their heads, loops through their ears, and little pretension of upward social mobility. By contrast, the contemporary interest in portraying blacks realistically and without bias is evidenced by the black dolls produced by such firms as Creative Playthings (Page D, #4) and Mattel. Mattel's "Talking Christie," first patented in 1965, is a Barbie counterpart. Her nostrils are accurately, but in no respect disproportionately, flared; her lips are full, but hardly to the point of exaggeration. She has a sophisticated hair style and clothes that are sleekly fashion-conscious, a far cry from grass skirts and bangle bracelets, which served in the most simplistic terms as reminders of African tribal rites on some of the earlier black dolls.

Two particularly desirable black dolls, again of an earlier era, are the Steiner child (Page F, #4), head marked "Paris A 78," and the unmarked, 13-inch (33-cm) French with brown sleep eyes, a closed, two-toned mouth, and ball-jointed, composition body (Page F, #5). Of the two, the unmarked doll has more decidedly Negroid features, including full lips and only imperceptibly flared nostrils. The Steiner black has typically Steiner features, including the crisp "v" points on the upper lip, and the long, slender fingers. She has well modelled, pierced ears, the original, tightly curled mohair wig, and heavy brows of an owlish thickness reminiscent of Jumeau. Of added interest is the 2¾-inch (7 cm) black all-bisque baby doll she is holding in her left hand (Page F, #4). This tiny example has a closed mouth, painted features, and bare feet (always considered a collector plus among all-bisque enthusiasts). She is dressed in a blue crocheted outfit with gold braid, complemented by a straw hat with gold-braid edging.

Another black doll conceived, like the Jumeau, from a stock mould is the winsome, 12-inch (30.5-cm) Hilda baby (Page F, #6). Marked "245 JDK jr. 1914 c. Hilda," she has the original mohair wig falling in bangs over her eyes. The eyes are also of the sleep variety, and her mouth is open to reveal two tiny, upper teeth. The Hilda baby has always been a collector classic. Since far fewer of these dolls were ever produced in the black than in the pale-complexioned version, this is a very choice doll.

Café au lait flesh tones on the 14½-inch 36.8-cm) Belton (Page F, #7) indicate that the maker intended her to represent a mulatto. Her slightly downcast open-closed mouth gives her an almost pouty look. She has pierced ears, set brown glass eyes, and her original lamb's wool wig. The lashes and brows are finely feathered, as is typical of French facial decoration. Her ecru dress with red trim, and her brown leather shoes are original.

CHINAS

Although chinas represent good buys on the current market, the truly desirable examples

Dolls made out of rubber have a naive charm which many collectors find appealing. Their tendency to collapse in the middle, however (note doll at left), is a drawback.

1

2

3

Since all-bisque dolls are generally small, the specialist in this area is at an advantage. A large number and variety of them may be displayed within a limited space. Subtle differences in facial expression and in body type are apparent in the grouping represented here.

4

5

Pairing a large, "big sister" doll with a smaller doll invariably adds interest to a specialist's collection, whether the paired dolls be striking Orientals or "cafés au lait."

1

2

3

4

5

6

7

A close look at this representative assortment of French and German black bisques reveals that manufacturers varied in the degree of realism with which they portrayed the facial features and skin tones of these dolls. Since black dolls were produced in fewer numbers than others, they are generally harder for today's collector to find and more expensive to purchase.

in this, just as in every other doll category, have always been relatively expensive. Nevertheless, most of the chinas pictured in this section would sell today for a great deal less than similarly choice French *bébés*. There has not as yet been a collector stampede on china-head dolls. Now would be a good time to acquire them. Before proceeding to do so, however, it would be advisable for the collector to become familiar with a few basic pointers about chinas. The better examples, like the "Eugenia" featured in Figure 63, were generally made in the middle years of the nineteenth century, or very shortly thereafter. These are the chinas that collectors admire and value for the elaborate detailing of the hairdos, as well as for the delicacy and expressiveness with which the facial features have been painted. The cheeks, as in the case of the Eugenia, are lightly rouged, the eyes are defined by red upper liners, and the nose is accented by tiny nostril dots. Collectors also accord special value to chinas which incorporate such unusual features as inset glass eyes, or exposed, pierced ears.

Figure 63.

Figure 64. Reverse side of Eugenia head, showing snood.

By contrast, the later chinas often seem lacking both in expressiveness and detail. The facial features may be bluntly executed, giving the doll a vacant, vapid look. Such dolls appeared by the millions during the 1880's and 1890's. Because of the manner in which the hairdo extends over the forehead in loopy waves, collectors refer to these late-edition chinas as "low brows." Because of their generally inferior quality and great abundance, they are also called "common heads." Occasionally, they are misleadingly dubbed "1880's chinas." The collector should recognize that many examples of this type were made after the 1880's period. The Butler Brothers were producing their "Pet Name" series china heads during the early part of the twentieth century (Figure 65). A tendency on the part of collectors to date chinas on the basis of hairstyle is therefore suspect. There is no concrete evidence that manufacturers discontinued the production of successful dolls simply because one aspect or another of ornamentation had become slightly dated.

A beginning collector might also be unduly impressed by the white yoke with its gold trim on the "Pet Name" doll, or by the raised gilt lettering which spells out "Dorothy." However, these are standard features and do not raise the value of such dolls at the present.

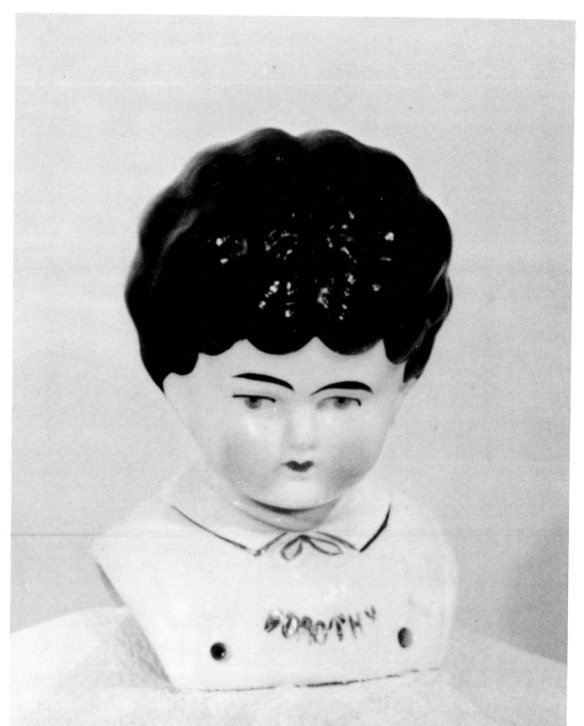

Figure 65. Turn-of-the-century "Pet Name" dolls such as this one were manufactured in vast quantities.

On the other hand, features which elevate the Eugenia in value are the moulded pink and white feathers outlining a black snood, and her flat, bootlike shoes. Flat shoes, as opposed to shoes with heels, are still another indication of an early china.

The distinguishing features of the 9-inch 22.9-cm) china shown in Figure 66 include the hairdo with center part. Wings of hair are drawn over the ears, extending back to a braided bun. She also has flat shoes, china forearms and lower limbs, and is dressed in her original two-piece outfit with pink fringe and ribbons. Her cheeks are lightly rouged, and the facial detailing, including nostril dots and eyeliner, is exceptionally fine.

Figure 66.

Figure 67.

Figure 68.

Another desirable china is the 10-inch (25.4-cm) example with gold snood (Figure 68). White and gold moulded ribbons outline the front of the snood, which is set off by the moulded blue bow. She has black hair with a high, center part, blue eyes but no liner, and nostril dots. Black hair, incidentally, is far more prevalent than blond on the early chinas. Blond-haired examples began to appear with ever greater frequency during the 1880's and continued in popularity until after the turn of the century. Note the high placement of the pupils on this doll. Often, but by no means always, this is an indication of an early china. Her brown-and-white-striped cotton dress is cinched at the waist with ribbon.

While the soft bodies on china-head dolls were frequently handmade and stuffed at home, manufactured cloth bodies did appear throughout the nineteenth century. One of

Figure 69.

the best known and highly regarded manufacturers was Philip Goldsmith of Cincinnati, Ohio, whose corset-bodied doll stuffed with sawdust and cattle hair became a commercial success in the mid 1880's. The 24-inch (61-cm) blond china, #2 on page H, with its well-defined, random curls, blue eyes with liner, and brown brows, is mounted on an unmarked, Goldsmith-type body. The red corset, red stockings, and black shoes with tassels are part of the body; however, on this doll the corset appears at the front only. The doll has plump shoulders with three sew-holes front and back. She is dressed in an early, but not original dress with cherry-colored flowers on a light, olive-green background.

The china depicted in Figure 70 has the desirable brown eyes, black hair with the high center part, and exposed ears. Ten well-defined sausage curls encircle the back of her head. The features are clear, and sharply rendered. Notice the slight upturn to the mouth, which gives the face its bemused expression. She has red eyeliner. The patent date of October 6, '69 is stamped onto the muslin body at the buttocks. Her high kid boots with tassels and buckles are stitched onto the body. Notice also the shaping of her hands (Figure 71), and

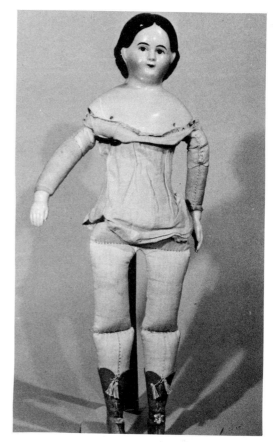

Figure 70.

Figure 71.

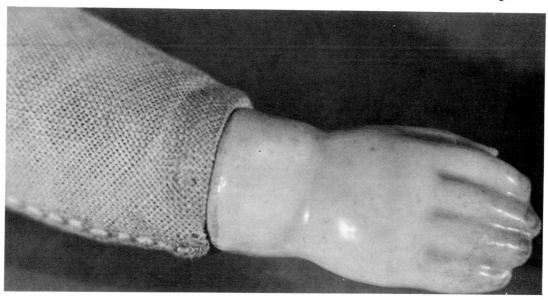

the manner in which the hands go in at the wrists. China dolls frequently have both china forearms and lower limbs, but sometimes the limbs are of cloth or kid, or even of some combination of materials. For example, the forearms might be of china while the lower limbs are of muslin.

The diversity of materials which have been used to cover chinas and to stuff them may amaze the new collector. Homemade china doll bodies, in particular, may also seem crudely assembled and bizarrely out of proportion to the rest of the doll. Experienced collectors find such variations intriguing. They recognize that one of the rewards of specializing is the growing awareness of the many ways in which dolls of the same type or period, or even of the same manufacturer, may differ slightly from one another.

The 6½-inch (26.5-cm) china depicted in Figure 72 is a small treasure. Her best feature consists of the extra-long, moulded curls which fall in an even cascade from the temples and entirely ring the back of her head. She has an unusually high center part, delicately applied features, and deep shoulders. The replacement clothes consist of green-and-peach-striped silk with lace ruffs at the bodice and sleeves. Her arms and legs are of china, and she has flat-heeled, black boots.

A few chinas do appear with wigs, but by far the most came with the moulded hairdos collectors typically associate with this doll type. The generalized use of human hair, or of cheaper substitutes such as lamb's wool attached to the original, animal-skin base, did not attain widespread popularity within the doll industry until the last three decades of the nineteenth century.

Figure 72.

FRENCH LADY DOLLS

So elaborate were the wardrobes and accessories that often accompanied the choicest French lady dolls of the 1860's and 1870's that contemporary observers became concerned. Critics pointed out that something must be wrong, possibly even sinful, with the lavish attention that was being devoted to dolls. What would happen to the values of children, to say nothing of adults, who became preoccupied with so much materialistic splendor?

Splendid indeed were the French dolls of this period. During the 1870's in Paris, dressmakers worked from dawn until dusk, painstakingly turning out gowns for dolls with an attention to detail rivalling that accorded the clothing of adult ladies of fashion. A well-dressed doll, such as those outfitted by the Maison Huret or by Mme. Lavallee-Peronne at her shop on the Rue de Choiseul, came with a dazzling array of bonnets and parasols, purses and pins, combs and brushes, slippers, shoes, and gloves. (See Figure 73.) Often, the cost to the buyer of acquiring the complete doll wardrobe could exceed by several times the initial cost of the basic doll.

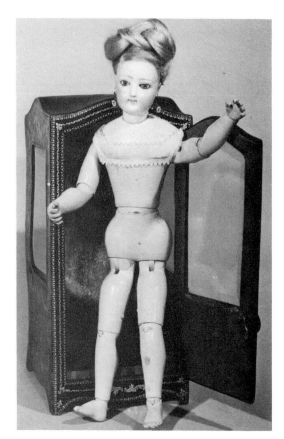

Figure 74.

Figure 73.

Many of the lady dolls associated with this production era were assembled on stitched, kidskin bodies. The dolls today considered to have been the more expensive editions at the time came with kid over wood bodies, or with meticulously articulated, all-wooden bodies. The 14½-inch (36.8-cm) unmarked lady doll illustrated in Figure 74 has this kind of body articulation. In addition to the jointing at the shoulders, elbows, wrists, and knees, the doll is also jointed at the waist and the ankles. This allows virtually limitless positioning possibilities, a factor which must have delighted its original, Victorian-era owner as much as it delights today's collector. The bisque head swivels on a bisque shoulder plate, as is characteristic of the finer 1870's examples. She has pierced ears, light blue, threaded-glass eyes, and a blond, mohair wig.

Figure 75.

Figure 76.

An interesting variation in body construction, although not unusual for costlier dolls of the 1870's, is pictured in Figure 75. The kid body has stitched toes and jointed, wooden arms. This 15-inch (38.1-cm) lady doll also has the pierced ears, luminous blue, threaded-glass eyes, and a braided blond mohair wig. The smiling mouth is a decided asset, as is the unusually pale and cream-textured bisque on the swivel-head and attached shoulder plate.

There has long been confusion in the doll world concerning the proper reference for these kid-bodied and wooden-bodied dolls. Collectors dubbed them "fashion" dolls, and a confusion in terminology persists to the present day. Technically, as conscientious researchers have always maintained, the word "fashion" suggests a function of a doll rather than a type of doll. Any doll, be it a child or a lady doll, could represent the fashions of a particular country or historical period.

The use of dolls of various types to portray fashions goes back many centuries. Surely the Victorian dolls dressed as ladies, with garments extending to the floor or sometimes just to their boot tops, personified the height of Paris fashion then. Essentially, however, such dolls were meant as playthings and seldom served exclusively as fashion models. One proof is that although elaborate wardrobes and accessories were indeed available in Paris for purchase along with the dolls themselves, the dolls which have survived in their original boxes are invariably unclothed, or accompanied by incidental ornaments only—a silk ribbon for the hair, a tiny choker for the neck. Since the available extra clothing was expensive, it was good business strategy to offer the basic doll

Figure 77.

at a moderate price and lure the buyer into spending more afterward.

The 26-inch (66-cm) unmarked lady doll shown in Figure 77 has a cloth body with kid arms. She has the bisque swivel-head on a bisque shoulder plate; blue, threaded-glass eyes; applied, pierced ears; and a blond, human-hair wig. Note the fine and typically French feathering of the upper and lower lashes, as well as the extremely pale blush tones to the cheeks. Her closed lips are turned slightly downward, giving the face its pensive expression. She is dressed in striped satin, accented with velvet and lace inserts.

Two additional lady dolls highly worthy of the specialist's attention include the 22-inch (55.9-cm) example illustrated in Figure 79 and the 17-inch (43.2-cm) example dressed in black mourning outfit (Figure 78). Both dolls have the typical, gusseted kid body with the bisque swivel-head and attached shoulder plate. The fingers on each pair of hands are separately stitched and wired, a feature common to the kid lady-doll bodies of the period. Collectors

Figure 78.

109

Figure 79.

often find that the kid has become stained in the finger area as a result of the gradual rusting away of the wire inserts. Advanced collectors prefer to leave the damaged hands on such dolls just as they are, rather than to replace or recover them. The blond mohair wig on the doll in Figure 79 has the original stitching used by the manufacturer to keep the long, sausage curls in place. Although her replacement clothes hardly do her justice, she never-

theless presents a haughty, aristocratic appearance. By contrast, the lady doll in mourning dress (Figure 78) has a much softer, more relaxed facial expression. This may be because her brows are not as dramatically arched. Whatever the reason, the considerable variety of faces as well as of body-types among the French lady dolls, adds incentive to collect them.

CHARACTER DOLLS

In 1909, the popular German firm of Kammer & Reinhardt introduced a "new" type of doll so unlike the idealized, sweet-faced dolls that the public had grown accustomed to that retailers were at first justifiably nervous about placing it on display. This doll, with its realistic, lifelike facial features and posable, five-piece "bent-limb" body, caught on quickly, however, and in succeeding years Kammer & Reinhardt, better known to collectors as "K*R," produced an entire series of such dolls. They called the dolls in this series *character dolls*, and gave to many of them an appealing name as well as the usual stock number. K*R named their first character "Baby," and numbered it "100." Collectors refer to this doll as the "Kaiser baby," the result of an early but mistaken impression that the doll had been intended to represent the infant German Kaiser.

It had a well-modelled bisque head with painted eyes, an open-closed mouth, and was available in a dark as well as a pale-complexioned version.

Kammer & Reinhardt was not the only firm to produce these dolls during the next decade, which corresponds to the period of the dolls' greatest popularity. As soon as it became evident that character dolls had captured the public's fancy, competitive firms including Heubach, Kestner, Simon & Halbig, and to a limited extent, Armand Marseille, jumped onto the production bandwagon.

One of the most familiar of the K*R character dolls is the 101, named "Marie." The doll came in different sizes as well as body types. The version in Figure 80 has the straight legs with painted-on sandals and stockings, the original dark blond wig with "doughnut" braids, and brown, intaglio eyes. A companion doll bears the name "Peter."

Figure 80.

111

Figure 81.

1

These early-twentieth-century dolls, with their impish, highly stylized facial features, represent a departure from the idealized, "dolly" faces of late-nineteenth-century production. The enormous popularity of the Kewpie doll inspired its appearance on a wide range of household objects, from novelty glassware to utilitarian cups and saucers.

2

3

4

5

The faces of some dolls create unforgettable first impressions. The modern doll artist, Bramble, has created a romantic beauty (upper left). In sharp contrast is the prim, purse-lipped beauty of the blond, moulded-hair china doll. A slightly downcast mouth heightens the soulful, dreamy look of the Heubach Köppelsdorf black baby. The large, expressive eyes and smiling lips of Madame Alexander's Scarlett O'Hara, on the other hand, lend an unmistakably aristocratic look to this striking doll.

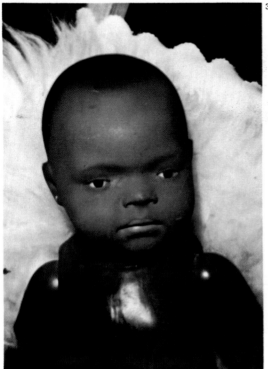

The K*R characters with the slightly sulky, slightly surly facial expressions are called "pouties." The number 114 pictured in Figure 81 first appeared in 1910. Named "Hans," he came with a sister doll of the same mould designation. The sister K*R 114, named "Gretchen," appears with greater frequency in collections, and is much coveted, as is Hans. The Hans shown here stands 14 inches (35.6 cm) tall, has the intaglio eyes, a light brown mohair wig, and is mounted on a jointed, composition body.

An interesting character variation is the K*R 115 A (Figure 82), with brown sleep

Figure 82.

eyes, closed mouth, and original golden-brown mohair wig. Like the 114, this example measures 14 inches (35.6 cm) and is on a jointed, composition body.

The K*R 121 is one of several K*R character dolls commonly found on the bent-limb-baby body. Many of these have the flirty eyes, as does the example featured on page G, #5. Some researchers have speculated that the bent-limb-baby body may have made its first appearance on the K*R 100, but there is no actual proof of this. The 121 baby shown here has blue-grey eyes, a curly, human-hair wig, and the characteristic dimples.

A particularly appealing character doll in the K*R series is the 116 A with its merry, laughing face, open-closed mouth with moulded tongue, and grey sleep eyes. This 15½-inch (39.4-cm) example is on a toddler body with straight wrists (Figure 83). An "S&H" marking incised at the back of the head directly before the 116 A indicates that this is one of the many character-doll heads made for K*R by Simon & Halbig.

The Heubach firm also produced a wide variety of character dolls, and some collectors limit their specialization to just these. The 14½-inch (36.8-cm) Heubach character shown in Figure 84 has the Heubach marking

Figure 84.

Figure 83.

on the back of the head in the form of a square. An alternative and equally prevalent Heubach marking was a sunburst. The example shown here has glass eyes, rather than intaglio ones. Intaglio eyes are typical of Heubach dolls, most particularly of their smaller ones. This doll also has an open-closed mouth with moulded tongue, and is dressed in early, but not original, clothes.

An interesting body variation appears on page B, #2. It is a transitional type, with bent-limb kid legs attached to a body which is also of kid. The arms have the conventional jointing and the forearms, as well as the shoulder plate, are of bisque. The bisque socket-head has the square Heubach marking, and the character face has an open-closed mouth, showing tongue and teeth. The intaglio eyes glance to the side. While it might be tempting to conclude that this somewhat awkward-looking assemblage is a put-together, such is probably not the case. Early Kestner character-baby heads are also found on bodies similar to this one, but with composition rather than kid lower legs. (See page D, #2.)

Still another well-known Heubach character is "The Whistler," shown in Figure 85. The doll is so-named because of the formation of the mouth, which is moulded into a puckered, whistling position. A voice box mechanism within the doll produces a whistling sound when the body is pressed. This example measures 14¾ inches (37.5 cm), has blue-grey intaglio eyes, and bears the square Heubach marking. The body is of cloth, with composition forearms.

Figure 85.

Figure 86.

The two-toned mouth on the Heubach character in Figure 86 is open, revealing two teeth and a tongue, both of which are moulded on. She has the laughing face with dimples so popular among the collectors of character-doll types, blue sleep eyes, and a blond, human-hair wig replacement. She stands 20 inches (50.8 cm) tall and is on a jointed, composition body.

By the early 1900's the French doll manufacturers had consolidated their forces in an attempt to compete with a soaring German doll production. While the attempt was not successful, in that French dolls after 1900 seldom equal in beauty or in artistry the finest pre-1900 editions, some of these dolls, notably the character types produced in series with the "S.F.B.J." marking, have great appeal. The S.F.B.J. pictured on page D, #5 is on a bent-limb-baby body and has the open-closed mouth with moulded tongue and teeth. Known among collectors as the "laughing Jumeau," the doll bears a 236 mould number (right side of picture).

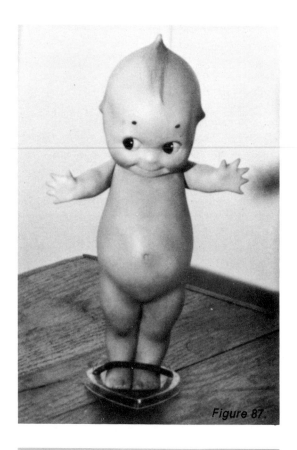

Figure 87.

Also desired by today's collectors are the so-called googly-eyed dolls of the sort produced by Kestner and Armand Marseille shortly after the turn of the century. Dolls with eyes that glance to the side have appeared throughout the history of doll manufacture, but the early twentieth-century examples, with their bulging cheeks and spoon-shaped mouths (often referred to as *watermelon mouths* by collectors), have an appeal all their own. Truly, they are less character in type than they are caricatures, for their impish faces reflect the whimsical in design, rather than the strictly realistic. It is in the context of such whimsy that Rose O'Neill fashioned her first Kewpie dolls, instituting a collecting mania that began with the American debut in December, 1912, and that has yet to show signs of abating. Some of the most popular Kewpie collectibles, as well as the most desirable, are illustrated in Figure 87 and page G, #1, 2, & 3. Collectors should note that "action" Kewpies, meaning those Kewpies moulded onto bisque chairs, or embracing, or holding bisque cats, suitcases, or umbrellas, are currently regarded as figurines rather than as dolls. These Kewpies, which go by such collector-assigned names as the "huggers," "Governor," and "Traveler" are nevertheless highly collectible and much in demand among Kewpie enthusiasts. For a glimpse into the life of an innovative twentieth-century doll artist, *The One Rose*, by Rowena Ruggles, is the definitive biography of Rose O'Neill.

Figure 88.

Typical of the googly-eyed dolls which have current collector appeal is the example featured in Figure 88. Marked "GB 253 Germany A 6/0 M," this 9¼-inch (23.5-cm) Armand Marseille has blue glass eyes, a brown mohair wig, and is on an inexpensive moulded body with moulded shoes and socks.

Another Armand Marseille googly is the popular "323," shown in Figure 89 with blue eyes, a blond mohair wig and a curved, though well-defined, upper lip line. She is 10 inches (25.4 cm) in height.

The A.M. 253 variation shown in Figure 90 is also 10 inches (25.4 cm) and has brown eyes and a blond, mohair wig. All three of the googlies which appear in this section have composition forearms with straight wrists.

Sometimes character dolls represent such

Figure 90.

Figure 89.

extremes of types that they have a special, though limited, appeal for collectors. Two such examples are shown in Figure 91 and Figure 92. The first of these has a bisque head mounted on a jointed, composition body and stands 15½ inches (39.4 cm) tall. His brown glass eyes are of the set variety, and he has an open mouth with teeth, and also has moulded brows. The heavy expression lines on the forehead and face, including the v-shaped lines between the brows and the parallel lines on either side of the mouth, have been fired into the bisque. He wears an original outfit consisting of a tri-cornered hat and three-piece suit. His head has the horseshoe marking.

The other, similarly dressed, unmarked character gentleman is also all original. He wears a tri-cornered hat, velvet and silk vest, and contrasting outer jacket and trousers. The quality of workmanship on the facial structure surpasses that of the companion doll, for the expression lines are more precisely moulded, and the features in general more sharply rendered. He has a beak-shaped nose, in contrast to the pug nose seen in Figure 91, a more protruding jaw line and chin, as well as more pronounced cheeks. His blue eyes are set, and his open mouth reveals an even row of teeth. The bisque head is mounted on a jointed, composition body.

The two dolls that close this section on character examples serve to emphasize a point which is occasionally lost upon new or over-eager collectors. With unusual dolls going for high prices today, it is tempting to elevate the worth of a doll whose expression is at only slight variance with that of a stock mould designation by dubbing it a "character," or a "character type." While in the final analysis there may be dolls which defy precise classification, the collector should be cautious about paying an elevated price for a doll, simply because the seller feels that some fine point—high placement of the eyebrows, or eyes that seem to "smile"—justifies the term "character."

MODERNS AND COLLECTIBLES

Modern and collectible dolls offer a wide range of specialization. Many collectors spe-

Figure 91.

Figure 92.

cialize in the celebrity editions, particularly those produced during the 1930's and the early 1940's. Among these, the Shirley Temple doll reigns supreme. First appearing in 1934, the Shirley was the most coveted, as well as the most imitated, doll of her day. While some of the Shirley look-alike dolls have merit in their own right, serious collectors opt for the fully marked and tagged Shirleys which the Ideal Toy Company produced in a variety of sizes, with a variety of outfits.

The two examples here, a 1930's composition Shirley (Figure 93), and a modern (1970's) Shirley in vinyl (Figure 94), are representative. The 25-inch (63.5-cm) composition Shirley is all-original and in mint condition. This one is marked "Shirley Temple Ideal" at the back of the head, with the size number be-tween the shoulders; however, Shirley Temple dolls vary considerably in the manner of marking. Sometimes the word "Ideal" appears without the name. Sometimes the name "Shirley Temple" appears on the torso without the size number. Size numbers also may be imprinted on the insides of the doll's arms or on the inner thighs. Occasionally, an authentic unmarked Shirley comes to light. These do not command the prices of the marked and tagged versions. In fact, unless a doll is clearly marked "Shirley Temple" on the head it will not command a premium price, even if the doll is tagged Shirley Temple and is wearing a "genuine Shirley Temple doll" dress.

While vinyl Shirleys by Ideal began appearing on the market as early as 1957, the vinyl examples of the 1970's are particularly

Figure 93.

Figure 94.

striking and, to many collectors, capture Shirley's dimples and her smile even more realistically than do any of the earlier dolls. The vinyl shown in Figure 94 has rooted synthetic ash-blond hair, stationary, hazel eyes, and smiling mouth with painted-in teeth. Marked "1972 Ideal Toy Co," she stands just over 16 inches (40.6 cm) and is in her original clothes.

Figure 95.

Other celebrities to appear in doll form include Sonja Henie and Deanna Durbin, both film stars of the late 1930's and early 1940's. The 21-inch (53.3-cm) Deanna in Figure 95 is marked "Deanna Durbin, Ideal Doll" and is all composition, with dark-brown, human-hair wig, sleep eyes, and an open mouth with teeth. She is dressed in a plaid flannel skirt with a green velvet jacket. The skates she wears are later additions and are not entirely suitable.

The 21-inch (53.3-cm) marked Sonja Henie

(Figure 96) is an Alexander doll. She has her original blond, human-hair wig, brown sleep eyes, an open mouth with teeth, and a dimple in each cheek. Her outfit consists of a navy skirt with white blouse and an embroidered vest. Her fingers show traces of the original pink nail polish, and she wears the characteristic skates. Composition Sonjas, like this one, came in varying sizes between the years 1939 and 1943. A re-issue in hard plastic and vinyl appeared during 1951. Like the Shirleys, the Sonjas came with an extensive wardrobe. Items of clothing could be purchased separately.

Figure 96.

A close-up of the Sonja (Figure 97) reveals a flaw that is a great problem with the dolls of this era. In the course of time, the eyes have a tendency to dim, taking on a splattered effect which is present here. Sewing machine oil ap-

Figure 97.

Specializing in the Alexander dolls has become an increasingly popular trend among contemporary collectors. The doll pictured on page H, #4 is a modern, 1978 version of Scarlett O'Hara. The Scarlett dolls, which Madame Alexander launched in the late 1930's, began with beautifully gowned composition editions. These later evolved into the hard plastics, and finally into the current editions in vinyl. Acquiring the many different Scarlett examples could most certainly form the basis of a collector specialty. Each of the Scarletts evidences meticulous detailing, the outfits on many of them representing Alexander costuming at its highest level of achievement. This one shows a satin gown with pink and red roses on an ivory background. The parasol and matching sash are a vivid green. Scarlett wears a ring and

Figure 98.

plied from time to time restores the color intensity.

For the collector with an eye toward investment, there are celebrity dolls of a more recent vintage than those just described. Such notables as Diana Ross, Cher, Marie Osmond, Loni Anderson, among many others, have been celebrated in doll form, and these modern dolls would be worthy of acquisition. They are, at the present time, still quite reasonable in price.

Among doll manufacturers, Madame Alexander has become a legend in her own time. Many of today's collectors are surprised to learn that she began producing dolls as early as the 1920's. What is more, early Alexanders were soft-bodied, cloth dolls with hand-painted facial features. From the beginning of her career, Madame Alexander has served as both innovator and guiding force within her doll company, personally supervising the production of each new doll from its initial design to its final costuming. Many collectors contend that for sheer inventiveness and for dedication to artistry, Madame Alexander's career in the twentieth century rivals that of the brothers Jumeau in the nineteenth.

pendant, as well as a straw hat with flowers and streamers. Her eyes are green, with the lids shaded a soft, delicate blue. She measures 21 inches (53.3 cm).

Madame Alexander changed from composition to hard plastic production in 1948. Typical of the Alexander dolls in the newer idiom was the 15-inch (38.1-cm) Alice in Wonderland depicted in Figure 98. Dating from the early 1950's, she came in three size ranges. This Alice wears her original blue taffeta dress, white stockings, and black shoes, but the same doll also came in a peach-colored dress. She has a closed mouth and green, sleep eyes. Like Scarlett, Alice is an example of a doll which Madame Alexander issued in one medium and then reissued in another. The first Alice appeared in a cloth version. The doll

later came out in composition, and after that in the plastic. The various editions could form the nucleus of still another collection of Alexander doll types.

The practice of making dolls for limited release is one which manufacturers observed as many as a hundred years ago. Collectors of antique dolls have always considered that the Jumeau incised "B. L." was originally intended for sale exclusively through the Louvre department store in Paris, the "B. L." thus standing for *Bébé Louvre*. Madame Alexander has also, from time to time, issued dolls under select circumstances. A modern example is the 7-inch (17.8-cm), marked and tagged Alexander which became available in the spring of 1980 as an exclusive of the Enchanted Doll House of Manchester, Vermont (Figure 99).

Figure 99.

The difference between the modern special-edition dolls and those produced many years ago is that nowadays manufacturers are well aware of the collector market and cater to it blatantly. Collectors who ordered the Alexander Enchanted Doll, for example, received a signed and numbered affidavit stating that the doll's initial issuance would not exceed 3,000 copies (Figure 100). Such documentation, unthought of many years ago, is designed for investment protection and represents the kind of business acumen which abounds in the contemporary doll world.

The Effanbee Doll Company has been creating the limited-edition dolls since 1974. In fact, Effanbee was the first manufacturing company to think of establishing a doll club for the specific purpose of alerting collector-members concerning upcoming releases. For 1980 Effanbee offered a delightful likeness in vinyl of the famous comedian, W. C. Fields. For 1981, Effanbee offered a 17-inch (35.6-cm) vinyl John Wayne doll, complete with saddle, carbine, and cowboy hat. Collectors concentrating on the modern special-edition dolls are growing rapidly in number.

There is a considerable amount of overlapping of doll types within the province of any specialized collection. The collector of character dolls, for example, may amass a number of blacks and Orientals along the way. Indeed, the ultimate satisfaction for the specialist in dolls comes from pursuing a dominant collecting theme and from finding as many different dolls as possible which are representative of that theme.

Figure 100.

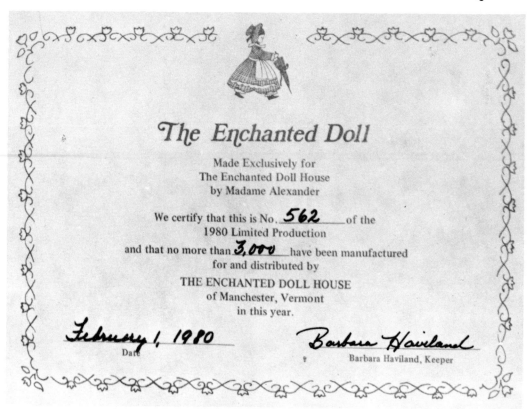

The Enchanted Doll

Made Exclusively for
The Enchanted Doll House
by Madame Alexander

We certify that this is No. *562* of the
1980 Limited Production
and that no more than *3,000* have been manufactured
for and distributed by

THE ENCHANTED DOLL HOUSE
of Manchester, Vermont
in this year.

February 1, 1980
Date

Barbara Haviland
Barbara Haviland, Keeper

Figure 101.

✎ 6 ✎

Repairing and Restoring Dolls:

Antique and Collectible

You have just acquired an early doll from a private owner, a flea market, or the musty attic of a departed relative. Your initial enthusiasm is so great that you temporarily overlook the shabbiness of her clothes, the soiled face, the matted wig, and the broken finger on her right hand. This is a doll that has not seen the light of day for many years. She rests in your arms now, worn with the passage of time and the extensive handling of children long grown to adulthood.

Your collector instincts suggest to you that she is a later bisque. Her open mouth with teeth, her "dolly" expression, as well as the ball-jointing of the body all confirm this. A quick check of her incised markings reveals a mould number and the telling word, "Germany."

Although you do not ordinarily acquire a doll of this type or in this condition, the price is low. The doll could conceivably become a good trade-off doll at some time in the future. In addition, something tells you that with a little time and effort on your part, you can repair her. The wig and the clothing appear to be early, perhaps original. The challenge of working on her intrigues you.

If you are a collector with both time and patience, there is much that you can do yourself to restore a doll, without giving her over to a professional. While it is inadvisable to clean the delicate velvets, laces, and silks often used to create the costumes of early dolls, sturdier fabrics in good condition lend themselves to cleansing in mild soap and water. Never use bleaches or detergents on any doll clothes. Invariably these prove too strong for fabrics which may, even at their best, be in a somewhat weakened condition. The surest way to test the fabric if you have any doubts about it is to pull gently at an inconspicuous spot, such as an upturned hem. Obviously, if the fabric begins to fray under slight pressure, it is wise to leave the garment alone. Once the doll clothes are clean, air dry and then lightly press with a steam iron. Ironing will restore the original crispness and life to most fabrics.

While you have the doll undressed, go over the surfaces with a soft cloth to remove dust particles. A mild solution of soap and water will prove effective on bisque, but you must take special care around the eye, ear, and mouth areas to avoid seepage. For cleaning these areas, use moistened cotton swabs. Paste wax as a cleanser is preferable to soap and water on composition dolls. Such wax will also help to retard crazing. Do not use powder cleansers on dolls; these can be quite abrasive.

Refurbishing a matted or tangled human-hair wig first involves its careful removal from the doll's head. Peel up gently from all sides until the wig comes loose. Never yank at a wig, for if it has been glued into place you may find that you have pulled away minor clumps of bisque from the edges of the crown, as well as from the wig itself. A wig may be easy or difficult to remove, depending upon how it was originally attached. On some dolls, generally the French ones, the wigs are simply pinned to a cork pate. If the wig refuses

to yield to the pressure of your fingers, dab some warm water on a piece of cotton and again peel up gently, applying the warm water to one portion of the wig at a time. Assuming that the glue is water-soluble, the wig will eventually pull free. If it does not, slow and careful work with an X-Acto knife will accomplish the job. When working with the knife, it is important to angle in, rather than to dig in, so as not to damage the base of the wig or the outlying head surfaces. Once you have removed the wig, you may use nail-polish remover to loosen remaining traces of glue.

Before shampooing any doll wig, be certain that you know whether the wig is human hair, mohair, or some other substance. Human hair lends itself well to shampooing. Mohair, on the other hand, does not. If you are shampooing a human-hair wig, first use a comb to work out the tangles. The coarse steel combs sold in pet shops are admirable for this pur-

Figure 102. Measuring a doll's head.

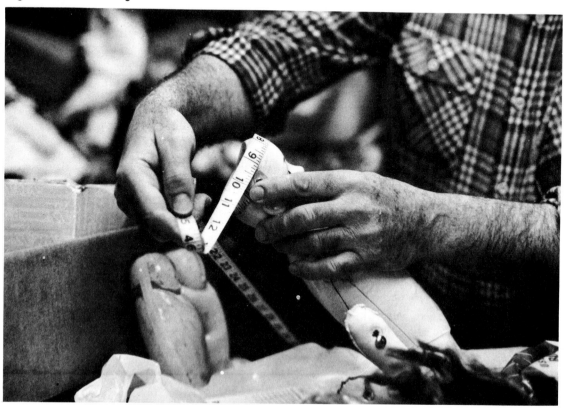

126

pose. While combing, press the hair to the wig base so that the pressure you are applying with the comb will not loosen or detach the hair. Comb only small sections of hair with each stroke. Do not try to comb the whole wig all at once.

While many professional restorers use liquid shampoo to cleanse the hair once it has been combed out, this generally involves removal of the wig base, if it is of cardboard, to avoid moisture-rot. Dry shampooing, although a bit difficult, is a safer and an equally effective method. If you do decide on a liquid shampoo, use a combination of extra-mild soap and cold water, pinning the wig to a wig block or to a plastic foam ball of the correct size, to prevent buckling or shrinking during the drying. While the wig is still wet, stretch the lining gently. It has some give, will not tear, and will stretch to the proper size.

On the subject of doll wigs, many collectors become adept at refurbishing them. It takes both patience and skill to weave in new hair or fibre in the worn spots so that the added material blends inconspicuously with the original. Most experienced collectors prefer to leave old wigs alone rather than to alter them, however. They often use hats or ribbons or hair combs to hide the problem areas. Of course, simply combing and shampooing can often greatly enhance a wig's appearance.

When examining the body of your doll, you will almost inevitably find scuff marks. Possibly there will be areas where the paint has cracked or chipped. Resist the temptation to repaint the affected areas. It is unlikely that you will be able to duplicate the exact color or texture of the original, despite your best efforts to do so. A thin application of white glue will prevent the damage from spreading and will not discolor the adjacent finish.

A slightly more complicated repair, but one still within the capability of the moderately skillful collector, involves the replacement of broken fingers on composition doll bodies. The first step is to drill a small hole into the exposed surface at the point of breakage. Next, cut a fine wire, curving it to coincide with the contours of the other fingers on the same hand. Also try to match the curvature of the corresponding finger of the opposite hand, providing of course that that finger is still intact.

When measuring the wire, be certain that it is slightly shorter than the finger will be, to allow for the added bulk of the covering material. Fill the drilled hole with epoxy glue mixed with a soft, malleable putty or plastic wood. Then insert the wire, and let it set. Apply putty mixed with the white glue to the wire frame with a fine brush, a thin layer at a time, allowing each layer to dry thoroughly before applying the next. Two layers are often sufficient. Once the final layer of the putty is dry, or "cured," to a dull lustre, slightly wetting the dried surface will render the repaired finger flexible enough so that you can give it its final shaping.

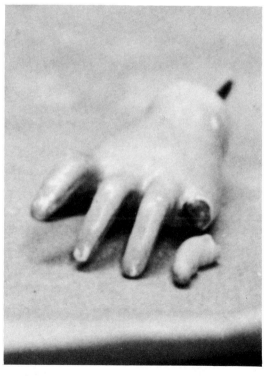

Figure 103. At the New York Doll Hospital, Irving Chais repairs a broken finger. The following six pictures show the operation in progress. An appropriately shaped piece is chosen for the finger.

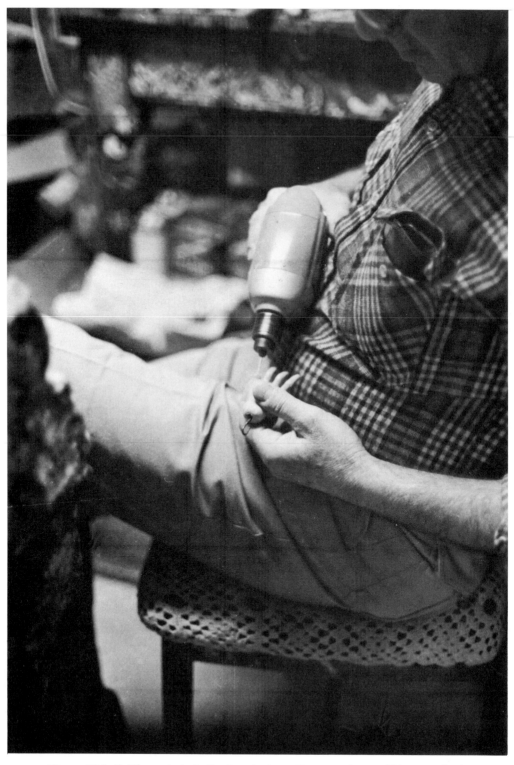

Figure 104. Drilling a hole in the hand where the new piece will be attached.

Figure 105. Fine wire inserted into the hand, to anchor the replacement finger.

129

Figure 106. Trying out the replacement finger.

Figure 107. Bending the wire, to position the finger correctly.

Figure 108. Gluing the replacement finger in place.

You will find that the skin-toned paints available in most hobby shops will serve for the application of the final color and sealer. Apply the paint sparingly with a fine brush to avoid unsightly gobs or paint build-up. A thin coat of lacquer mixed with tint (satin, semi-gloss, or gloss) will seal in the paint and create a reasonably accurate color blend with the surrounding areas. If the rest of the hand is rough or slightly crazed, avoid giving too slick a finish to your repaired finger. Since minor flaking should simply be sealed with a thin application of glue to prevent future damage, it may seem contradictory to suggest painting the restored fingers. The reason is simple. A small amount of flaking on a doll body is seldom disconcerting; moreover, the body is almost invariably clothed. A rebuilt finger which has been left roughened and untinted is a distracting eyesore.

Although repairs of this kind are quite standard, no two professionals work in precisely the same way, or use precisely the same combinations or proportions of glues, putties, or sealers. A finely detailed account of a method of finger restoration quite similar to the one just described appears in the outstanding doll repair book by Marty Westfall, *The Handbook of Doll Repair and Restoration.*

Irving Chais, owner of the New York Doll Hospital, however, uses a different approach for rebuilding fingers. He begins by selecting an appropriately shaped piece of finger from his large supply of doll parts. After inserting fine wire into the portion of the finger remaining on the hand, he glues on the new piece of finger. He then carefully files off the excess glue and paints and shellacs the finger to achieve the desired color and lustre. Therefore, the repaired finger is of the same basic material as the rest of the hand, and is also of the same time period.

If you happen to possess a doll of little value, you can experiment with the various mending materials until you come up with the formula that works best for you.

While the general procedures for restoring plastic and vinyl dolls are similar to those

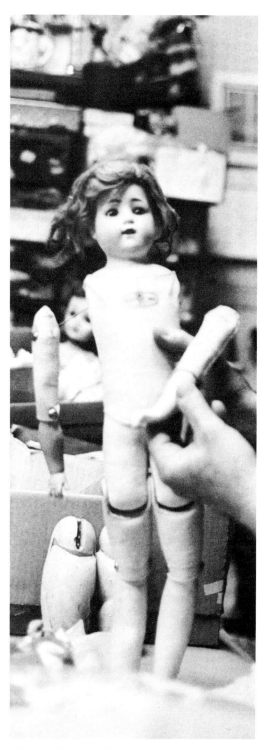

Figure 109. A doll in for repair because the arms have come off.

133

which prove effective in restoring the bisques, chinas, and compositions, there are certain differences.

Spotting and staining is much more of a problem on plastic and vinyl dolls than on earlier bisques and chinas, simply because these later materials, especially vinyl, have a far greater tendency to absorb foreign matter. Ink stains on vinyl dolls prove resistant to mild soaps. Plain Mercurochrome works better, as Patricia Smith has noted in her Modern Collector's Doll series. After application of the Mercurochrome, apply cotton that has been soaked in household bleach and then squeezed dry. This will help remove stains from your vinyls.

Irving Chais suggests that it is risky to try to remove dried ink, and that it is preferable just to regard the stain as a beauty mark. Ink that has not set and been absorbed into the plas-

tic can be removed with mild soap and water.

Another product that works with some success on ink stains is the stencil-ink removing paste sold in office supply stores. It is mild, safe, and effective, providing you are careful to remove all residues once the stain is gone. Care must of course also be taken to see that cleaning fluids do not seep into facial openings or into the wig. This is as important a factor on plastic and vinyl dolls as it is on bisques or early compositions.

There is, of course, no limit to either the amount or kind of restoration work a collector with talent can do. The collector who mends doll fingers usually learns to restring dolls. Some collectors even manage to master the art of china repair. Those who wish to learn more about these processes should certainly consider the possibility of becoming professional doll restorers. Most professional

Figure 110. Rebuilding a leg joint.

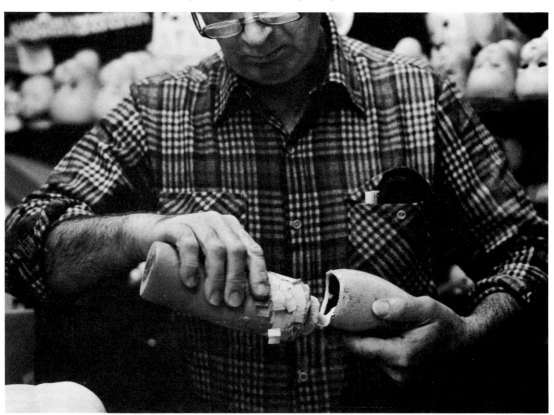

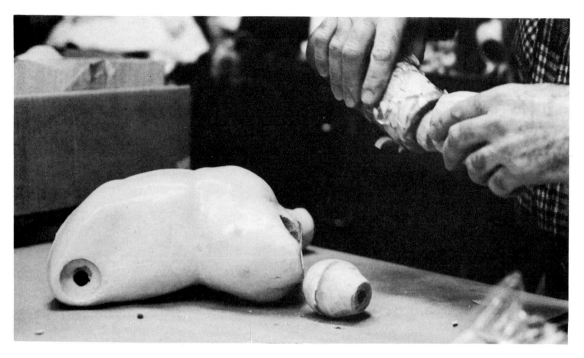

Figures 111–112. Gluing leg joint and reattaching repaired leg to doll body.

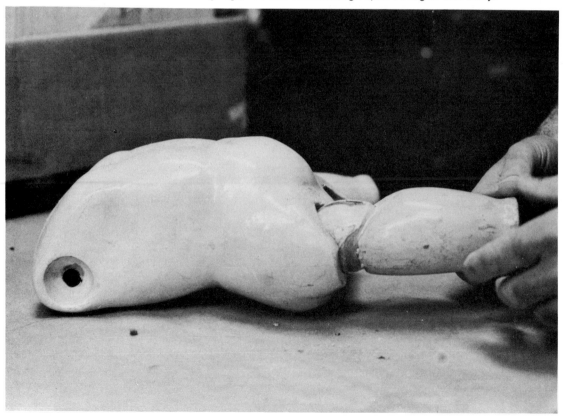

restorers began their careers with simple experimentations on dolls acquired primarily for collecting purposes.

If you do not have either the interest or the patience for such work, you should still be aware of today's standard precepts concerning doll restoration. No mending materials, for example, should ever be so strong that the mend cannot at some future date be taken apart again, should this prove necessary for any reason. Nor should any doll restoration work be disguised, rendering it impossible for you or a future collector to ascertain the original damage. While it is perfectly acceptable to mend the head of a bisque doll, the mend should be skillful enough to be virtually invisible *on the outside*. Smearing plasters or sealing putties all over the inside of the head to obliterate or disguise the telltale repair areas is strictly unprofessional.

Additionally, when cementing porcelain, bisque, or parian, be sure that the parts are perfectly united. If they are glued unevenly, the glue will not be absorbed and a perfect union will then be impossible.

Another point about current doll repair has to do with the many excellent putties, sealers, and glues now on the market. While some of these materials work admirably on dolls, it is always advisable to use materials as closely related as possible to the original substances used to manufacture the doll. If you are not sure about a particular glue, paste, or adhesive, test it first on an inconspicuous spot (or on something other than the doll you are repairing), to avoid doing damage and creating additional work.

The restorer must also be thoroughly familiar with the repair materials, and know in advance to what extent the substances used may in time change in texture, firmness, or color. There is little value to repair work that is good-looking upon completion but in the course of time alters, so that color or texture distinctions are apparent between repaired and original areas on the doll.

There will inevitably be some differences anyway in bisque repair between original,

Figure 113. *This Shirley Temple look-alike is an excellent example of how a bad restoration job can look worse than no restoration at all. The face has been too highly finished and the wig is a poor-quality synthetic.*

kiln-fired decorative work and the layers or coatings of whatever paints and related substances the contemporary restorer applies. Old bisque cannot be refired successfully. Therefore, the restored areas will always be more susceptible to damage than the original areas. The doll must be handled with this in mind—still another good reason for keeping careful records concerning the nature and extent of repairs on any doll. The effects anticipated on a restored doll should also be given careful

Figure 114. Sanding a
doll body. Try to do doll
repairs in well-ventilated
areas. Note exhaust fan
in this picture.

Figure 115. Painting a doll body.

You must also be certain in advance that the chemical composition of whatever materials will be used on a doll will not have an adverse effect. Certain substances will melt vinyl or plastic rather than mend it. A professional certainly should be thoroughly familiar with restoration materials in order to avoid such a possibility. If you are working on a doll yourself, however, you may be tempted to save yourself time by combining ingredients that are used in two distinct steps for a particular type of doll restoration. What you may little realize is that the combined ingredients could prove lethal. I would not combine even so apparently harmless a substance as white glue with another mending agent without first knowing the possible results. This philosophy would apply to work on any doll, old or recent. White glue, by the way, is useful in keeping cracks from spreading in just about any kind of doll, regardless of its period of manufacture.

While on the subject of safety, remember to use paint and flammables in well-ventilated areas only. Never smoke while using these materials.

Most contemporary doll restorers abide by the rules devised for museum restorations countless years ago. The basic precept is to return the object to its original condition without changing the object from its original condition. Restore only those portions of the doll it seems absolutely necessary to restore. Leave the rest alone. An overdone restoration may actually diminish the doll's value and detract from its appearance. Before you have any doll that you own professionally restored, it is a good idea to examine previous examples of the restorer's handiwork. It is also a good idea to observe the extent to which various types of dolls now a part of museum collections have been restored.

Remember, by learning all you can about the basics of restoration—as well as by observing the techniques employed by experts—you will be in a better position to make informed decisions about damaged dolls which you deem to be worthy of acquisition.

consideration in relation to the techniques the restorer wishes to use to achieve the effects. If the only way to restore the tooth of a doll involves a process that might prove detrimental to the original mouth paint, it would undoubtedly be best to leave the tooth alone. Disrupting one part of a doll to repair another is always of questionable value.

7

Selling Dolls:

The Collector as Dealer

Sooner or later almost every collector parts with a doll or with a group of dolls. The collector may simply have tired of a particular doll or doll type, and may sell some dolls in order to obtain the funds necessary to strike out into new collecting territory. A collector who has been accumulating dolls for some time may look back upon early purchases with a sense of nostalgia, mingled with chagrin. The early dolls no longer represent either the quality or the level of sophistication of later acquisitions. Or a collector may have to part with prized dolls in order to cope with an unanticipated financial emergency.

There are several options available to anyone who has dolls to sell and wishes to reap the highest possible profit. These options include placing advertisements in doll periodicals, responding to "dolls wanted" ads in these same periodicals, submitting the dolls to shops willing to take them on a consignment basis, or calling in local dealers or collectors—particularly those who know the seller and are already aware of the contents of the collection. Doll hospitals are quite naturally likely buyers

for dolls in poor or damaged condition, as are doll restorers, most of whom advertise that they buy, sell, and trade dolls in addition to mending them.

Since the climate in which a collector sells dolls is often an emotionally charged one, it is important to plan a strategy carefully, taking one step at a time. Selling in haste or in panic invariably results in poor financial returns.

The first piece of advice for the collector-turned-seller is: Know your dolls thoroughly. If you have not been purchasing dolls recently, and have not kept up with the going prices, consider calling in a professional appraiser. Price books, as has been mentioned elsewhere, are fine indicators of approximate rates. But in addition to being slightly out of date even as they are being prepared for publication, the prices quoted may not accurately reflect the worth of your particular dolls.

A knowledgeable appraiser will be able to tell you how much to expect for a doll, given its particular merits. The appraiser will suggest how much you should take off for certain kinds of damage, or how much you should add on for all-original clothing. If you have a large group of dolls to sell, the appraiser may charge a flat rate, and then an additional amount for every hour or day required to complete the work. The results in terms of eventual sales can make the expenses involved well worthwhile.

If you plan to sell dolls from your home, it is best to call in just one buyer at a time. You will find that most dealers and collectors will meet your price if the prices assigned are reasonably equivalent to the going rates.

Tagging each doll with a brief identification and price is the most sensible procedure. Avoid asking prospective buyers to make offers on your dolls. Some collectors and most dealers consider this a veiled strategy for securing a free appraisal. The pricing of the dolls is en-

Figure 116. Matched pair of Kestner character babies seated in Victorian doll's trunk.

Figure 117. These stamped-metal miniature doll strollers with elaborate filigree work are typically Victorian.

tirely up to you. If you find that a particular purchaser wishes to buy several of your dolls —or possibly all of them—it is also up to you to decide whether or not to give a discount on the total amount involved. Some buyers like to bargain. A few may even speak disparagingly of your dolls in an effort to get you to lower your prices. If you know the worth of your dolls, as well as their desirability, there is no reason to succumb to such pressure. On the other hand, several dealers customarily offer more than the asking price, when buying at a collector's home, when it becomes apparent to them that the value of the dolls has been grossly underestimated.

Provide any buyer who leaves with a doll with a sales slip, briefly describing the doll, its defects, if any, and return privileges, if you wish to allow them. Most home sales are final. A statement to this effect should also be written on the sales slip.

If you would rather not engage in the sale of your dolls directly, placing them on a consignment basis, either with a doll dealer or with a dealer in general antiques, may prove to be equally effective. There are several reasons why it is preferable to entrust your dolls to a doll dealer, rather than to a general dealer, however. While the general dealer may occasionally handle dolls, it is unlikely that his experience with them is equal to that of an established doll dealer. A person who deals exclusively in dolls will be well aware of the market for your dolls, may already have clients for some of them, and is in a better position than the general dealer to reach the doll-buying public. The dealer may include your dolls in photo display ads if he does mail-order business, or bring them to the doll shows and conventions to which he is regularly invited.

Financial terms must again be arranged between you and the dealer. Often the dealer will ask you what prices you have in mind for your dolls and will agree to sell them at your price. There must, of course, be some leeway for dealer mark-up. The dealer is entitled to a fair profit for his services as your sales representative. If he feels that the prices you quote are too high for him to realize a profit, he will tell you so. It will then be up to you to remain firm or to lower your prices to accommodate the dealer. If you have had the dolls appraised prior to your transactions, you will know the extent to which you can come down in price and still realize respectable returns on your merchandise.

Realize, however, that once you begin advertising dolls, you are functioning as a dealer. As such, you may need to obtain a certificate of dealership and pay a fee. If you are in doubt about where to obtain the certificate, your local town or city clerk will advise you. While the initial fee is minimal, most states require you to fill out forms periodically, indicating the status of your sales. Failure to comply with state regulations can result in financial penalties. There are dealers who boast that they have never bothered with such regulations.

Figure 118. Open-mouth doll with moulded brows.

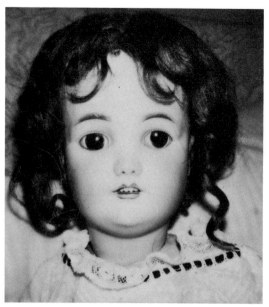

Figure 119. Thirty-three-inch (82.5 cm) Heinrich Handwerck doll.

You may feel affronted by the suggestion that you adhere to them scrupulously. "After all," you may be saying to yourself, "I really have just these few dolls to sell."

The fact is that most of today's dealers got their start in precisely such a manner—by advertising their unwanted dolls in dealer periodicals. It is a small step from one successful doll advertisement to the active buying and selling of dolls as a full- or a part-time business. Should this indeed happen to you—should the initial sale of a few dolls from your collection induce you to acquire additional dolls for the express purpose of selling them at a profit —sooner or later you may even find yourself renting space at doll shows.

Customarily, a dealer more established in the business will recommend you for a particular show, or to a particular show manager. The most popular shows, as well as the most elite ones, are extremely selective about dealers. It could conceivably take years before you were deemed eligible for shows of a certain calibre. Bear in mind also that participation in any doll show involves certain requirements. You must first sign a contract with the show manager.

WHAT TO BRING TO A DOLL SHOW:

MASTER SUPPLY LIST FOR DEALERS

Bring the following to each show:

1. The dealer-manager contract, proving your authorization to participate in the show.

2. Doll stands in sufficient quantity and in the sizes needed for dolls you plan to display.

3. Table coverings, if not provided by manager.

4. Folding tables, if not provided, or extra tables, if needed and permitted.

5. Price tags (*extra bag* of large-sized ones). All dolls should be tagged with prices and pertinent descriptions prior to the show.

6. Disposable diapers, to wrap dolls you plan to exhibit.

7. Banana-shipping cartons, to store dolls in transit from your home to show. (They are better than other cartons, because they generally have an opening at either end, which functions as a handle.)

8. *Sturdy* bags in *large* sizes and several packages of tissue paper, for packaging dolls sold at show.

9. Dealer business cards, if you use them.

10. Receipt books for recording sales.

11. Petty-cash box and approximately $10 in loose change.

12. Table lamps or floodlights, extension cords.

13. Pens, transparent tape, masking tape.

14. Wooden risers and supporting stands.

15. Thumb tacks, rubber bands, paper clips.

16. A thermos of hot coffee (you will want a cup before the manager has it ready for you).

17. A very small first-aid kit, including aspirin!

18. The directions to the show!

While contracts do vary, most include a stipulation absolving the manager from complete responsibility for your dolls during the run of the show. The contract will also require you to pay all of the participation fee, or a portion of it, in advance. This fee is generally determined by the calibre of the show and the amount of booth space you select or are allotted.

If the show is a small one that is not yet firmly established, you may also be required to provide your own set-up tables and covering cloths. Additional props, such as risers to set off your dolls at varying levels and spotlights to lend added illumination to your booth, are always up to the dealer to supply. So too, of course, are travel and motel expenses if the show is an appreciable distance from your home and two days' duration or more. Experienced dealers take all such matters in stride. Aside from the sales which may develop during show hours, the dealer and collector contacts, as well as the doll leads which often materialize, can more than compensate for the time, the effort, and the expense of participation.

Should you indeed find yourself selling your dolls at shows, prepare a master list of props and supplies you will need, and attach this list to a clipboard. Double-checking the list before you depart for the show will ease the way. You can also avoid the embarrassment of having to run from dealer to dealer, at your first shows, asking for the items you overlooked.

Many collectors and dealers sell either individual dolls of merit, or entire lots of dolls, through auction houses. It stands to reason that if auctions are good sources for buying dolls, they are also good outlets for selling dolls. Ms. Pamela Brown of Sotheby Parke Bernet, Inc., in New York, offered both shrewd advice and sound reasoning on this subject.

"Auctions," she pointed out, "serve as a good barometer for the doll market. The prices at which dolls consigned to us sell are the real prices dolls are fetching on the current market. In fact," she added, "dealers make

Figure 120. Full portrait of china discussed on page 104.

it their business to follow our auctions closely, so that they can better determine the prices they should set on their own merchandise." Ms. Brown, head of the Collectibles Department at Sotheby Parke Bernet, personally guides the people who come to the gallery seeking information about dolls they have to sell, as well as people seeking advice about buying dolls. "Our auction gallery sends its catalogues all over the world. We reach an international group of collectors and dealers.

"The gallery is on the seller's side, in the sense of wishing to share with the seller the benefits of broad competition for merchandise."

This competition is elicited not only by advance-of-auction catalogues, but also by extensive advertising of the sales, and by assertive public-relations strategies. I have known of collectors who have shied away from auction houses, fearing that their dolls would be mishandled, or possibly even lost or stolen. Sotheby Parke Bernet is typical of auction houses now selling dolls in a thoroughly responsible manner.

Unless otherwise covered by the seller, insurance at Sotheby Parke Bernet costs $6.00 per $1,000 of the gross sales price. Furthermore, during the pre-sale exhibition of the dolls, which at Sotheby's runs anywhere from three days to one week, examination of the dolls is strictly on a one-to-one basis. A guard will remove from the display area the particular doll a prospective buyer wishes to see, supervise while the buyer is handling the doll,

Figure 121. Paper party masks show Dorothy and her friends from the Land of Oz. They would represent a prize for the collector of the Judy Garland doll.

and then return the doll to its appointed place.

Absentee bids on dolls are accepted by the gallery, with detailed descriptions given over the telephone to callers seeking more specific information about the dolls than the catalogue may contain. "I will describe every speck, every flaw I find," Pamela Brown added. "I know that people who cannot come in to see the dolls for themselves need added reassurance before sending in bids." It is the gallery, incidentally, which sets the value on the dolls for sale at each auction. The commission for the gallery is 10 percent of the selling price for a lot that brings more than $500 at auction, and 15 percent for a lot that fetches $500 or less. Dolls at auction bear a contractual minimum, protecting each doll to 60 percent of the pre-sale estimate. This means that there is a respectable price below which the gallery will not release a doll to a bidder.

"Don't make major repairs on dolls you plan to leave for auction," Pamela Brown advises. "Collectors prefer to supervise all of that themselves." She does advise, however, spending the $25 or so to restring a doll which otherwise would present a limp, bedraggled appearance.

After the sale, the seller can expect a check from the gallery in about thirty-five days, according to Ms. Brown. "The check is for the full amount of the sale, minus the gallery's commission."

Ms. Brown also maintained that dolls are a viable investment during uncertain economic times. "The doll market has a broad base, regardless of the economy," she said. "It is a more stable market than many others."

Finally, Sotheby Parke Bernet has been singled out as a consignment location only because it is a well-established, honorable gallery, one where collectors receive the kind of courtesy and attention that they deserve. There are many other equally respectable auction houses in New York City and in other locations in this country and abroad.

Richard Withington's methods of conducting doll auctions, for example, involve courtesies as thoughtful as those extended to clients at Sotheby Parke Bernet. The high bidder on each doll receives the doll immediately, rather than at the end of the sale, and has several minutes in which to examine the doll thoroughly. If there is a valid difference between the condition of the doll and its condition as described in the auction catalogue, the buyer has the right to refuse the doll, thereby negating the sale.

There are many acceptable procedures for selling dolls. Auction houses are frequently a good choice. The heart of the matter is that collectors and dealers must decide upon the particular system, or combination of systems, that works best for them.

Figure 122. 1870's French lady doll, re-dressed.

Appendix

CHECKLIST FOR DOLL SHOPPERS

Some collectors improvise checklists to aid in decision-making while doll shopping. These vary according to the doll type, but they do have one important feature in common. They enable the collector to pinpoint in writing both a doll's assets and its shortcomings at the time of purchase. Filling out a checklist may be time consuming, but this process does help the collector to make a rational appraisal of a doll, rather than an emotional one. Looking at one's own written assessment of a doll's major faults definitely reduces the chances of an impulse purchase. A completed checklist belongs in the doll file, as a permanent part of a doll's history.

The checklist that follows might serve for a bisque-headed doll on a composition, ball-jointed body. The "x" marks and the commentary are hypothetical.

Item	Quality or condition				Comments
	Excellent	*Good*	*Fair*	*Poor*	
Wig	x				original, very full
Pate		x			original cork
Eyes and eye mechanisms			x		glass scratched at corners; sleep mechanism sticks
Facial paint (lashes, brows, mouth paint)	x				brows even, feathering light and fine; delicate mouth (two-tone paint)
Modelling of features: ears, nose, mouth				x	very little definition to ears (worn mould?)
Bisque surfaces		x			smooth, even-toned bisque; tiny chip on right eyelid
Composition surfaces			x		parts of body repainted—some color differentiation between new paint and old
Doll markings	x				clearly incised lettering at back of head
Stringing			x		loose—doll should be restrung
Hands			x		two fingers broken, left hand
Feet				x	several toes smashed
Ball-jointing	x				limbs move easily
Arms, legs, torso		x			some roughness at arm and leg openings
Clothing, including undergarments		x			all-original, but undergarments tattered and badly stained
General appeal		x			doll has particularly expressive face; this is an appealing doll for its type

GLOSSARY OF TERMS

ALL-BISQUES

Dolls, most often small, composed entirely of bisque. They may be jointed or unjointed.

ARTICULATION

A term collectors use with reference to the jointing characteristics of particular doll types.

BALL-JOINTING

A technique of jointing, employing balls of wood or other material attached to adjacent sockets of a doll's limbs, to afford flexibility of movement and a wide range of possible limb positions.

BÉBÉ

A term of French extraction, used with reference to dolls representing small children, commonly ranging from infancy to no more than seven years.

BELTON

The name collectors apply to bisque-headed dolls with from one to three stringing holes in the pate. Although an M. Belton was active, along with Jumeau, in nineteenth-century doll production, no doll specifically marked "Belton" has ever been located or conclusively identified.

BENT-LIMB

A reference to the curved limbs on the five-piece baby bodies which doll manufacturers produced shortly after the turn of the century.

BISQUE

Unglazed porcelain, customarily tinted, with a dull rather than a glossy patina.

BONNET BISQUES

Bisque-headed dolls decorated with bisque hats. Often flowers and bows formed a moulded part of the head itself.

CELEBRITY DOLLS

Dolls created in the likeness of well-known personalities.

CHARACTER DOLLS

Realistic-looking dolls, as opposed to dolls representing idealized conceptions of children. Character dolls, as most collectors today conceive them, date from 1909.

CHINA-HEADS

Dolls made of glazed porcelain, rather than the unglazed type. Often the bodies of such dolls are of cloth. China-heads were either pressed or poured into the mould, the pressed heads usually, but not always, of earlier manufacture.

COMPOSITION

A catchall term that collectors use with reference to dolls constructed of a combination of materials. Technically, any doll could be termed a composition doll. However, collectors today regard as compositions those dolls whose heads or whose entire bodies are made up of glue, rag, paper, and wood pulp, with some sort of varnish overlay.

CROWN OPENING

The cutaway portion of a doll's head. Manufacturers often left this open, not only to facilitate insertion of eye mechanisms, but also to reduce the doll's overall weight, and thus cut down on shipping costs.

DOLL

The word "doll" is a replacement for the earlier word "baby," used in Europe until the end of the seventeenth century, and in America until the middle of the eighteenth. By the late 1700's, the word "doll" was in popular usage. Dolls are figures, jointed or unjointed, that are meant to be playthings rather than to serve as miniature statues, party decorations, or figurines.

EYES, FLIRTY

Doll eyes that move from side to side and, in some instances, up and down as well, by means of weights.

EYES, GOOGLY

Doll eyes that look to the side. Characteristically, they are large in proportion to the rest of the doll's facial features. Also called "goo-goo" or "rougish" eyes.

EYES, INTAGLIO

Painted-on eyes, as opposed to inset glass ones, with slight indentations of the pupils.

EYES, PAPERWEIGHT

Eyes that have a heavy layer of clear glass over a colored base, giving them a lifelike effect.

EYES, SLEEP

Eyes that move back into the head as the doll is moved. Frequently, sleep eyes are operated by weights. Such movement usually reveals an eyelid which covers the eyes while the doll is "asleep."

EYES, STATIONARY

Eyes that are positioned into the head so that they cannot move. Also called "set" or "fixed" eyes.

FASHION DOLLS

A term collectors apply to dolls initially dressed in stylish clothing of their period or in the costume of their place of manufacture. While the French lady dolls were sometimes used to portray clothing styles, they were manufactured primarily to be playthings for children.

FROZEN CHARLOTTE

An unjointed bisque or china doll. Collectors have occasionally termed such dolls "pillar" dolls.

HARD PLASTIC

The heavy plastic some manufacturers used to produce dolls following the Second World War.

KEWPIE DOLLS

Elfin-like dolls, usually composed of all-bisque, created in the early twentieth century by the popular artist and illustrator, Rose O'Neill.

LADY DOLLS

Dolls constructed to represent an adult female.

MARKINGS

The symbols and motifs, sometimes difficult to decipher, which manufacturers use to identify their dolls.

MARKINGS, EMBOSSED

The raised letters and numerals that make up the markings on the back of doll's head, the shoulder plate, or elsewhere.

MARKINGS, INCISED

Markings that are pressed in, rather than raised.

MECHANICALS

Dolls capable of performing a variety of activities, from a single gesture to an elaborate sequence of gestures. The activating mechanisms are usually concealed within the frame of the doll.

NAME DOLLS

Dolls bearing an actual, manufacturer-assigned name, rather than a collector-assigned name. The tin-headed doll marked "Minerva" is therefore a name doll, as are the Shirley Temple doll and the Madame Alexander "Little Women" dolls.

OPEN-CLOSED MOUTH

In this type of mouth, there is a visual separation of the lips, sometimes revealing a moulded tongue and teeth. However, there is no actual opening for the mouth cut into the doll's head.

PARIAN

Dolls made of untinted bisque, with the features and hair representing the only areas of coloration. The word "Parian" comes from the Greek *Paros*, a city noted for its fine, pale marble.

PEDDLERS

Dolls, most frequently dating from the nineteenth or early twentieth century, that hold trays brimming over with miniatures of wares for sale. Peddlers were made of a variety of materials, including bisque, kid, and *papier mâché*. Those in their original glass domes and on their original bases are particularly desirable.

REPRODUCTION

A doll which is the product of a mould that the maker has created from a doll already in existence.

S.F.B.J.

These are the initials for *La Société pour la fabrication des Bébés et des Jouets*, the French doll concern organized in 1899.

SHOULDER-HEAD

The doll's head and shoulders comprise a unit of identical materials. For example, they are both composition. The head and shoulders of such dolls may be one piece, or they may show a separation at the neck. The shoulder-head is attached to a body of a different material. A bisque shoulder-head may appear on a kid body, or a china shoulder-head may appear on a cloth body.

SHOULDER PLATE

The shoulder portion of a shoulder-head doll, to which the head is attached. When there is a separation at the neck, enabling the head to "swivel" on the plate, as in the case of some early chinas and parians, as well as many of the French lady dolls, the value of the doll is frequently higher than when the head and shoulder plate form a single unit.

SOCKET-HEAD

The doll's head tapers into a neck joint which, in turn, fits securely into an accommodating socket at the shoulder top. The socket-head is movable.

STIFF WRISTS

Sometimes collectors refer to these as "straight" wrists or as "unbroken" wrists. In such dolls the forearms extend to the fingertips without a jointed separation at the wrist area.

TWO-TONE MOUTH

The lips of the doll are painted, and then outlined for contrast in a color that is usually slightly darker than that of the lips themselves.

WASP WAIST

The cinched-in waist, characteristic of some adult dolls.

BIBLIOGRAPHY

Angione, Genevieve; Whorton, Judith. *All Dolls Are Collectible*. New York: Crown Publishers, Inc., 1977.

Coleman, Dorothy S., Elizabeth A., and Evelyn J. *The Collector's Book of Dolls' Clothes*. New York: Crown Publishers, Inc., 1975.

———. *Encyclopedia of Dolls*. New York: Crown Publishers, Inc., 1968.

Foulke, Jan. *3rd Blue Book of Dolls and Values*. Riverdale, Maryland: Hobby House Press, 1978.

———. *4th Blue Book of Dolls and Values*. Cumberland, Maryland: Hobby House Press, 1980.

———. *Treasury of Mme. Alexander Dolls*. Riverdale, Maryland: Hobby House Press, 1979.

Fox, Carl. *The Doll*. New York: Harry N. Abrams, Inc., 1972.

Jacobsen, Carol L. *A Sentimental Portrait of Dolls*, Volume I. Paducah, Kentucky: Collector Books, 1979.

———. *A Past and Present Portrait of Dolls*, Volume II. Paducah, Kentucky: Collector Books, 1979.

———. *A Very Special Portrait of Dolls*, Volume III. Paducah, Kentucky: Collector Books, 1979.

———. *A Treasured Portrait of Dolls*, Volume IV. Paducah, Kentucky: Collector Books, 1979.

King, Constance. *Dolls and Doll's Houses*. London: Hamlyn, 1977.

McClinton, Katharine Morrison. *Antiques of American Childhood*. New York: Bramhall House, 1970.

Revi, Albert Christian. *Spinning Wheel's Complete Book of Dolls*. Hanover, Pennsylvania: Everybodys Press, 1975.

Ruggles, Rowena Godding. *The One Rose*. Oakland, California: Rowena Godding Ruggles, 1964.

Schroeder, Joseph J., Jr. *The Wonderful World of Toys, Games, & Dolls 1860–1930*. Chicago: Follett Publishing Company, 1971.

Schweitzer, John C. "Problems of an 1880's Toymaker." *Spinning Wheel*. Hanover, Pennsylvania: December, 1974.

Smith, Patricia R. *French Dolls: in Color with Current Values*. Paducah, Kentucky: Collector Books, 1979.

———. *German Dolls: Featuring Character Children and Babies*, Paducah, Kentucky: Collector Books, 1979.

———. *Modern Collector's Dolls*. Paducah, Kentucky: Collector Books, 1973.

———. *Modern Collector's Dolls*, Second Series. Paducah, Kentucky: Collector Books, 1975.

Westfall, Marty. *The Handbook of Doll Repair and Restoration*. New York: Crown Publishers, Inc., 1979.

INDEX